The Klausenberger Rebbe

The War Years

The Klausenberger Rebbe: The War Years

Translated and adapted by
Judah Lifschitz
from *Lapid HaEish* by Aharon Surasky

TARGUM/FELDHEIM

First published 2003
Copyright © 2003 by Judah Lifschitz
ISBN 1-56871-219-7

Published by:
TARGUM PRESS, INC.
22700 W. Eleven Mile Rd.
Southfield, MI 48034
E-mail: targum@netvision.net.il
Fax: 888-298-9992
www.targum.com

Distributed by:
FELDHEIM PUBLISHERS
202 Airport Executive Park
Nanuet, NY 10954

Printed in Israel

To our beloved children
and grandchildren

May the flame of the
Klausenberger Rebbe's torch
illuminate the paths of your lives

ב"ה

THE YESHIVA
OF GREATER WASHINGTON
Excellent Together!

ב' דר"ח כסלו תשס"ג
November 6, 2002

Lapid Haish is a biography of the famous Klausenberger Rebbe זצ"ל authored in Hebrew by Rabbi Aaron Sorsky. It is an exceptional work which portrays the life of this great צדיק and his many contributions to כלל ישראל.

We owe a debt of gratitude to Mr. Judah Lifschitz, a prominent attorney in our community, who has translated this outstanding work making it available to the English speaking public. Judah Lifschitz has gained a well earned reputation as a מזכה את הרבים in the Silver Spring Jewish community, for his leadership in צרכי ציבור and his many acts of חסד on behalf of the needy. This is the third book which he has translated thereby establishing a חזקה. May he be זוכה to continue his labors on behalf of כלל ישראל until ביאת גואל צדק במהרה בימינו.

בברכת התורה

Rabbi Gedaliah Anemer

Contents

Translator's Preface

A Jew can reach new spiritual heights only by connecting himself to a tzaddik, for it is through the tzaddik that one develops abilities greater than those which one can develop on his own.

(*Nesivos Shalom, Parashas Korach*)

Lapid HaEish, written by Aharon Surasky and published by Yechezkel Shraga Frankel, is the story of the awe-inspiring life of the Klausenberger Rebbe, Rabbi Yekusiel Yehudah Halberstam, *zt"l*. The original Hebrew text follows this great chassidic Rebbe from his birth on 4 Shevat, 1905, in Rudnick, Galicia, until his emigration from the displaced persons camps of post–World War II Europe to the Williamsburg neighborhood of Brooklyn, New York, in 1947. A second volume is anticipated to be published in Hebrew to record the Klausenberger Rebbe's extraordinary life and accomplishments in the United States and Israel from 1947 until his death on 9 Tammuz, 1994.

This translation, *The Klausenberger Rebbe: The War Years*, focuses on a major subset of the period chronicled in *Lapid HaEish*, beginning with the onset of World War II in 1939 and continuing through the Rebbe's efforts in the DP camps. During these years the Rebbe suffered through the brutal seven levels of Gehinnom and emerged to build anew not only his family, which had been completely destroyed in the Holocaust, but also Sanz-Klausenberg Chassidus and many important Torah institutions the world over.

Studying the life of a *gadol* is important because it brings with it the power to transform — a spiritual force which takes a willing reader from who he is to who he can become. Such study connects one with the tzaddik — his spirit, his teachings, his righteousness — and forever links the reader to him. Connecting to a *gadol* is critical because it is the *gadol* who enables us to attain our true spiritual potential. Thus, exploration of the compelling life story of the Klausenberger Rebbe, Rabbi Yekusiel Yehudah Halberstam, *zt"l*, means questioning the meaning of one's own life and committing oneself to a life of greater study of Torah, more careful observance of mitzvos, and a deeper awe of the Almighty.

I approached the writing of this book with both excitement and trepidation. Excitement for the opportunity of making available to the English-speaking public the incredible life story of the Klausenberger Rebbe, *zt"l*. Trepidation, for who was I to put into words the story of one of the greatest Torah scholars and Jewish leaders of all time? With the Almighty's benevolence and guidance, I was able to complete *The Klausenberger Rebbe: The War Years*, and for this I am eternally grateful.

Many have contributed, each in their own special way, to the publication of this book, and I appreciate all that they have done.

The publication of this volume would never have been possible without the tireless efforts and constant support of Rabbi

Heshy Turner, my devoted partner in this endeavor. My life has forever been enriched by Rabbi Turner's friendship.

Rabbi Aaron Lopiansky, *maggid shiur* of the Yeshiva Gedolah of the Yeshiva of Greater Washington, introduced me to *Lapid HaEish* and suggested that I read it. Eli Meir Hollander of Feldheim Publishers encouraged me to pursue the translation of the Klausenberger Rebbe's biography and was instrumental in making the *shidduch* for me with the Klausenberger community.

My wife, Marilyn; our children, Pirchie and Yosef, Nachum and Tamar; and our grandchildren, Moshe and Adina, are the inspiration for all my efforts. They provide me with never-ending support and I am indebted to each of them — knowing full well that I will never be able adequately to thank them for all that they do. May the life of the Klausenberger Rebbe, *zt"l*, inspire and motivate each of them to grow in the service of the Almighty and *klal Yisrael*.

My parents and in-laws, my brother, sisters-in-law, and brothers-in-law, and their families are beloved sources of support for which I am thankful.

My partners, Ron Shapiro and Steve Schram, are like brothers, and I am blessed to have them as both partners and friends. I am also most appreciative of all of the wonderful and highly talented people who are my professional colleagues and staff. My assistant Shannon Weiner worked very diligently (despite my handwriting) on the edits to the manuscript and contributed meaningfully to the publication of this book.

I have been privileged to be associated with the talented people at Targum Press for several years. The special efforts of

Moshe Dombey, my editor, Chaya Baila Gavant, and the staff at Targum Press were instrumental in developing my original concept for this book into what became *The Klausenberger Rebbe: The War Years*.

Silver Spring, Maryland, where I reside, is a community that teaches and inspires one to grow spiritually. I am thankful to its rabbis and leaders and particularly to the Yeshiva of Greater Washington for all that they have done *lehagdil Torah u'lehadirah*. I am indebted to my dear friend Rabbi Zev Katz for his constant encouragement and support of my writing.

I have the deepest admiration for my *mara d'asra, rosh hayeshivah*, and rebbe, Rabbi Gedaliah Anemer, *shlita*. He has inspired me to strive to become a true *ben Torah*. If ever I succeed in earning that appellation it will be as a result of the example he has set. May the Almighty shower His blessings upon Rabbi and Rebbetzin Anemer, *ad meah ve'esrim*.

I spend every evening studying the *daf yomi* with a dedicated group of friends. No matter what transpires during the day, the study of Torah with these individuals makes it possible for me to continue on to the next day. To each of them I offer my thanks.

Lastly, it is my fervent hope that *The Klausenberger Rebbe: The War Years* will inspire Jews everywhere, and particularly our youth, to greater Torah study and to the realization that by connecting to *gedolei Yisrael* a simple Jew can attain spiritual greatness.

May the memory of the Klausenberger Rebbe, *zt"l*, be a blessing for all of *klal Yisrael* and may it protect us all, and especially our brethren in the Holy Land, until the final redemption and the coming of Mashiach, soon and in our days. Amen.

Judah Lifschitz

Introduction

Rabbi Yekusiel Yehudah Halberstam was a rare and holy man. As the standard-bearer of Sanz Chassidus in the twentieth century, he was known in the Jewish world simply as the "Klausenberger Rebbe." With his great inner strength, he resembled the leaders of earlier generations; his sole purpose in life was to serve Hashem and His people.

The Rebbe was one of the few in his generation who merited to wear the three crowns of glory: the crowns of Torah, *avodah* (service), and *malchus* (royalty). His expansive knowledge of both the revealed and hidden aspects of Torah made him one of the greatest Torah scholars of his time. As a youngster he was identified as an *iluy*, a child prodigy, and an extremely diligent student. When he matured he received *semichah* from the outstanding rabbinic authorities of his time. He spent sixty years teaching Torah and expounding on halachah, responding to all who sought his opinion on halachic issues, and wrote a major work of responsa, *Divrei Yatziv*, on the four sections of the *Shulchan Aruch*.

In the realm of *avodas Hashem*, the Rebbe was known for his outstanding righteousness and holiness. His extreme dedication to Hashem and selflessness in performance of mitzvos enabled him to reach the apex of spirituality.

Adorned with the crowns of Torah and *avodah*, the Rebbe was blessed with royalty, *malchus*. He became the beloved Rebbe of dedicated chassidim, young and old, reminding them of his great-grandfather, the Divrei Chaim of Sanz. In his later years he became recognized as one of the leaders of the Jewish people, working for and carrying the burdens of the nation and fighting its spiritual battles. With his broad vision and perception of the world around him, the Rebbe was able to anticipate its diverse needs and work to fill them.

After the destruction of European Jewry in the Holocaust, the Rebbe devoted himself to establishing hundreds of institutions and organizations the world over, bringing both spiritual and physical salvation to his brethren. The Rebbe returned the Jewish people to its glory of old, in a fashion and to a degree that no one else could do. It is impossible to adequately describe his success and accomplishments in this area. The Rebbe was clearly a chosen representative of Hashem, sent to deliver a message of life and hope to the survivors of the Holocaust.

A Burning Torch

The Rebbe was dynamic, passionate, and intense. From the day of his birth to the day he returned his soul to his Maker some ninety years later, he was enveloped by his love of and desire to serve Hashem, His Torah, and His people. Anyone who came in contact with the Rebbe, for any period of time, saw clearly that he was afire. Enormous energy burned inside him, like lava in a volcano.

Shortly before his fortieth birthday, the Rebbe was subjected to the greatest of ordeals: the Holocaust. Only with Hashem's kindness did he emerge from the Nazi hell alive, cleansed, purified, and unsinged by Hitler's flames. The sacred fire in his heart continued to burn even after the extreme suffering he endured. It was present in everything he did, whether grappling with a difficult halachic issue, discussing Gemara with his students, spilling his heart out in intense prayer, conducting his *tisches*, speaking words of Torah to his chassidim, or traveling from place to place to spread the word of Hashem and increase the sanctity of the Jewish people.

It was said that the great leader Rabbi Shimon ben Gamliel would juggle eight burning torches in the Beis HaMikdash without them ever touching one another. In a similar fashion, the Rebbe handled many different torches in the spiritual darkness of our days. Each project he undertook was a torch lighting a path for the Jewish people to their Creator, and each was ignited by the fire that burned within his pure heart. Like Rabbi Shimon ben Gamliel, none of the Rebbe's projects interfered with or diminished the other. He was able to influence many Jews throughout the world to greater observance, and his sacred fire will continue to burn from the *batei midrash* of his followers until the coming of Mashiach, speedily in our days.

A Complete Torah

Every detail of the Rebbe's life is a complete Torah, to be analyzed carefully. When he was still a young boy, the greatest Torah scholars and spiritual giants of the era were deeply impressed by the scope of his knowledge and the sharpness of his intellect. After years of devoted study in yeshivah, where the Rebbe gained extensive Torah knowledge and served outstanding rabbis, he matured into a great scholar and tzaddik, though he was still unknown in the larger Jewish world.

During the nearly twenty years that the Rebbe served as the *rav* of the city of Klausenberg, the capital of Transylvania, he taught large numbers of students in the yeshivah he established and enjoyed a large following of chassidim. He led his community with a strong hand and also influenced many people who lived in other cities. During those years he lived as an ascetic, with his feet on the ground but his head in the heavens. His true greatness and extraordinary spiritual strength, however, remained hidden until the Holocaust and the period after the war.

During the Holocaust, the Rebbe went through a living hell. His torture and suffering began with his imprisonment in Budapest, Hungary's capital. Later he went into hiding in Klausenberg to avoid capture by the Nazis and their allies, then escaped to Banya, where he was imprisoned in a labor camp. At around this time his beloved wife and eleven children were murdered in the sanctification of God's Name.

The Rebbe was taken to the Polish valley of death called Auschwitz, and after a few months was transported as a slave laborer to Warsaw to clean up the ruins of the ghetto. Several weeks later, he was marched on a cruel and brutal seventy-mile death march toward Dachau. From there he was taken to a concentration and work camp in the forest of Muldorf. By open miracles, he survived each harrowing experience and lived.

Despite all that he went through, the Rebbe's spirit did not break, nor did his resolve weaken. He continued to live a life of Torah, mitzvos, faith, and holiness wherever he was transported and whatever the conditions of his imprisonment.

After the Nazis' defeat and liberation by the Allies, the Rebbe devoted himself with superhuman energy to reviving the Jews who emerged from the concentration camps and returning them to a vibrant Jewish life. Hidden abilities, extraordinary leadership and resourcefulness suddenly awakened within him. He rekindled the spark of Judaism in the masses of survivors, calling out in a clear and confident voice, "He who is for God, come to me!"

The Rebbe breathed new life into the downtrodden survivors. He gave strength to the broken-hearted and healed their wounds, caring for thousands of orphans and lonely souls who had no one left in the world. He was a loving father to them all. He fought against the oppressive hopelessness which gripped the survivors, renewing their faith, trust, courage, and hope. He organized the men, women, and children in the displaced persons camps into genuine, traditional Jewish communities. He established a network of yeshivos, Talmud Torahs, and educational institutions for girls. When the survivors were finally able to emigrate from Germany, he devoted himself entirely to their cause, establishing institutions for them in their new homes and involving himself in many other activities to strengthen their Torah observance and better their lives.

Restoring the Glory of the Jewish People

The Rebbe's greatest desire was to restore the Jewish people to their full glory of old. The institutions he opened educated a new generation in the ways of the Sanz chassidic dynasty, bringing it to the level of its predecessors in many ways. The Rebbe produced countless learned, God-fearing students, many of whom became Torah leaders. A community centered around a rebbe came to life once again, like the communities that had existed before the Holocaust in Galicia and Hungary.

The great fire from the days of the Divrei Chaim of Sanz returned to guide and warm the hearts of the faithful. From his home in Williamsburg, New York, the Rebbe's influence spread far and wide — to Canada, Mexico, Chile, and Eretz Yisrael. In the United States, he reestablished a community of Torah-true Jews, whose headquarters eventually moved to Union City, New Jersey.

In later years, the Rebbe moved to Eretz Yisrael, where he built yet another community from scratch. He established what would become his crowning achievement — a network of Torah institutions in Kiryat Sanz, a suburb of Netanyah, with a sister community in Yerushalayim. The network included Talmud Torahs, yeshivos, elementary schools and high schools for girls, kollels, nursery schools, and old age homes. In addition, he established the famous Sanz-Laniado Hospital in Netanyah, which is managed entirely according to halachah and enjoys a reputation for outstanding care, and Mifal HaShas, a program which can now be found in Torah institutions throughout the world.

The Rebbe was already in his sixties when he reached Eretz Yisrael, yet his drive was that of a young man just starting out in life. The holiness of the land invigorated him. He immersed himself in the study of Torah and gave deep and brilliant expositions on Gemara and halachah, deepening his students' understanding and encouraging them to grow and develop.

In his popular lectures on Chumash and Rashi, the Rebbe was a fountain of chassidic philosophy. He taught Hashem's word to all who longed to hear it. Anyone who heard the Rebbe daven and cry to his Creator, like a child who had misbehaved, was never the same again. It was well-known that spending Shabbos or *yom tov* with him was like experiencing a day in the World to Come.

The Rebbe opened his doors to all those who sought him out, comforting all the poor and troubled souls who flocked to him. Full of compassion, he poured prayers and blessings on those who asked his advice, soothed their hurt, and wiped away their tears. In addition, he beseeched Hashem to have mercy on his people. He defended the nation endlessly and tried to protect them from every enemy, whether it be in heaven or on earth. He argued on behalf of *klal Yisrael* and prayed for forgiveness and blessing, for the restoration of the *Shechinah*, and for the redemption of the Jewish people.

The Rebbe's heart continued to blaze with a burning love for Hashem which raised him to an almost superhuman level. Although he suffered from pain and disease in his later years, his spiritual strength enabled him to continue his heavy daily schedule without letup.

It was for good reason that young and old looked at the Klausenberger Rebbe with admiration and awe. His spiritual character, his life of complete holiness, and his great accomplishments were extraordinary. Even more incredible was his emergence from the concentration camps with the spiritual energy and strength to create new worlds and breathe new life into his fellow survivors. The Rebbe's life cannot be fully understood by mortal man. He was a gift from Hashem to a destitute nation, a persecuted and orphaned generation.

No one has ever entered the Rebbe's inner world to discover the source of his greatness and sanctity. This book highlights the Rebbe's extraordinary life of accomplishment but cannot possibly do justice to his humble spirit and broken heart. The visible aspects of his spiritual greatness are described in these pages and nothing else; the Rebbe succeeded in hiding from human eyes his true greatness. "In revealing a handbreadth, he hid two thousand *amos*."

Nonetheless, in that which was revealed there is more than enough for those who wish to study the Klausenberger Rebbe's way of life and his complete dedication to the Almighty and His people. We must only be sure to remember that, in truth, we cannot even touch the surface of his greatness.

9 Tammuz, 5757
The third *yartzeit* of the Klausenberger Rebbe
A. S.

Chapter 1

Before the Tragedy Struck

A Scion of Sanz Chassidus

Rabbi Yekusiel Yehudah Halberstam, the Klausenberger Rebbe, was a descendant of important chassidic families with roots in Hungary, Galicia, Poland, and Romania. His father, Rabbi Tzvi Hirsch, was a grandson of the Divrei Chaim of Sanz and of Rabbi Yekusiel Yehudah of Siget, known as the Yitav Lev. The Rebbe's mother, Rebbetzin Chaya Mindel, was a descendant of the Bnei Yissaschar, Rabbi Elimelech Shapiro of Dinov, and the Ateres Tzvi, Rabbi Tzvi Hirsch Eichenstein of Ziditchov.

Young Yekusiel Yehudah was born on 4 Shevat, 1905 (5665), in the town of Rudnick, Poland, where his father served as *rav*, as his father and grandfather had before him. Reb Tzvi Hirsch was a pillar of the Sanz Chassidus dynasty. Until Yekusiel Yehudah was thirteen, Reb Tzvi Hirsch was his primary teacher and role model.

As a Youth

From young Yekusiel Yehudah's earliest years, his father instilled in him Torah and fear of Heaven. When he was just three years old, Reb Tzvi Hirsch wrapped him in a tallis and carried him to the Rudnick cheder. There he presented him to the teacher of the youngest children, who began to teach young Yekusiel Yehudah the *alef-beis*. When the first lesson was finished, Reb Tzvi Hirsch again wrapped Yekusiel Yehudah in the tallis and took him home. The rest of the day, he watched over the boy and did not let him leave the house. The windows were shut and completely covered so that the three-year-old's eyes would not see anything improper in the street.

When Yekusiel Yehudah was a little older, he started to learn Chumash. The event was marked by a festive celebration attended by many guests and members of the community. Before the party began, young Yekusiel Yehudah, dressed in fancy clothes and adorned with gold and silver jewelry, was lifted onto the table where his father was sitting. As was the custom, he gave a short speech. When he finished, one of the guests asked him, "*Yingele*, what are you studying?"

"Chumash," the youngster answered.

"What is this Chumash?" the guest continued.

"*Torah tzivah lanu Moshe morashah kehilas Yaakov*," answered Yekusiel Yehudah.

"Who gave us the Torah?"

"HaKadosh Baruch Hu, who chose us as His nation from amongst all the nations and gave us His Torah."

The questioner continued, "And why is it called 'Chumash'?"

Undaunted, the boy responded, "Because in the Torah there are five books: *Bereishis, Shemos, Vayikra, Bemidbar,* and

Devarim." As he said the name *Devarim*, he thrust his thumb downward and upward like a seasoned Torah scholar.

His Father's Death

During World War I, the family was forced to flee Rudnick and settled in Kleinwardein, where they remained for six years. Rabbi Tzvi Hirsch passed away during these years, when his youngest son, Yekusiel Yehudah, was a mere thirteen. Despite being orphaned at such a young age, Yekusiel Yehudah learned a great deal from his saintly father: the fundamentals of Torah scholarship and the chassidic way of life, many chassidic ideas and philosophy, and, most important of all, his extraordinary character traits. Years later, the Rebbe would say of his father's influence, "Everything I heard and saw of my father remained etched in my memory forever. Even the things I witnessed when I was very young I remember well. I shall never forget a thing...not even a simple gesture of his."

Reb Tzvi Hirsch instilled in his son a love for the teachings of the Divrei Chaim. "All his life my father would talk about Sanz. Just as a person does not forget that he is alive, so my father did not stop thinking, even for a moment, about my holy great-grandfather the Divrei Chaim. But we did not hear stories of miracles. Rather, he would only tell us about the Divrei Chaim's way of serving Hashem — how he prayed and studied Torah, how he recited *Hallel*, how he conducted his holy *tisch*, what he would do before and after davening. All these things would teach us to serve Hashem."

After his father's death, Yekusiel Yehudah, already known as "the *iluy* of Rudnick," put all his efforts into learning Torah.

He studied with several great chassidic Rebbes, including the Imrei Emes, Rabbi Meir Yechiel of Ostrovtza, Rabbi Chaim Eliezer Shapiro of Munkatch (author of the *Minchas Eliezer*), and others. He also became acquainted with many of the greatest Rebbes of the time.

The Rebbe later explained his success in the study of Torah in the following way. "In my youth I was considered a bright and diligent student. How did I accomplish this? I tricked my *yetzer hara*. Other children made great plans at the beginning of the school year for the whole year, and in the end they failed. I said to myself, 'I am going to plan just for today and set goals for this day only.' The Satan, not being interested in a single day, left me alone. The next day I again made plans just for that day, and so on until the end of the year."

Marrying and Moving to Klausenberg

In 1925, at the age of twenty, Yekusiel Yehudah married Pessel Teitelbaum, the daughter of Rabbi Chaim Tzvi, the rabbi of Siget, known as the "Atzei Chaim." Pessel was also a descendant of the Divrei Chaim, since her maternal grandfather, Rabbi Shalom Eliezer of Raczfert, was his son. For the engagement, Yekusiel Yehudah's father-in-law gave him a gold watch, but the young groom sold it and bought a beautiful *Shas* instead.

For the first two years of his marriage, Yekusiel Yehudah remained in Siget, learning Torah from his father-in-law, who loved him dearly. Then, in 1927, he assumed the position of Rabbi of Klausenberg, the capitol of Transylvania (now Romania).

The Jewish community of Klausenberg had a long history,

dating back to 1591. In 1927 it boasted a population of 16,000 Jews, the majority of whom were irreligious and associated with either communist or Zionist groups. The Orthodox community was in a weakened state. Recognizing the gravity of the situation, a group of chassidic Jews formed their own minyan and hired Reb Yekusiel Yehudah as their rabbi.

Although he was perhaps the youngest rabbi in the country, Reb Yekusiel Yehudah made an immediate impact on his new community. His charismatic personality attracted even the more modern and less observant segments of the Jewish community. On his first Shabbos in Klausenberg, more than three hundred men came to daven with him and to attend the *tisch* he conducted. When he spoke on Shabbos HaGadol and Shabbos Shuvah and when he lectured on *Pirkei Avos* during the long summer days, he would speak for several hours to large audiences, including the less religious Jews.

The Rebbe's love for all Jews, including the nonreligious, was enormous. One Shabbos, as he walked down the street, a simple Jewish peddler, smoking a cigarette, called out to him sarcastically, "Good Shabbos, Rebbe."

Rather than becoming angry, the Rebbe answered softly, "Good Shabbos. What is your name? Perhaps you can join me for a *melavah malkah* tonight?"

The peddler, embarrassed, immediately started to extinguish his cigarette. But the Rebbe stopped him. "*Chas veshalom!* It is prohibited to put a cigarette out on Shabbos. Just put it aside."

In the end this peddler returned to his faith and became the Klausenberger Rebbe's *gabbai*.[1]

---

1 Reported by Pinchas Zelig Berger.

Dedicated Completely to Others

The Rebbe's salary, as those close to him knew him well, never entered into his mind. The entire time he served in Klausenberg, he lived in poverty. All his furniture was broken and the windows of his home were covered with cloth instead of curtains because the Rebbe gave all his money to the poor. Finally, the family's financial situation deteriorated to such an extent that the lay leaders of the Klausenberg secretly sought the advice of other great rabbis, who ruled that the community should give the Rebbe's salary directly to his wife.

For himself the Klausenberger was content to make due with the bare minimum. Often he gave his own meal to a hungry yeshivah student or guest, careful that his *rebbetzin* not see what he was doing. When he saw that an impoverished, ill, and starving man in the community was left unattended to because of his sickly appearance and body odor, the Rebbe personally took him into his home, fed him, and cared for him until he returned to health. Later in life, the Rebbe would credit this act of kindness with saving him from the crematoria.[2]

Immersed in Torah and Prayer

The Rebbe waged a constant battle against his physical and material needs. His daily schedule was not that of a typical man. He immersed himself in the *mikveh* frequently and denied himself the enjoyment of food and drink, eating bread only on Shabbos and holidays and often eating only one meal a day. He slept a mere three hours a night, often on a bench in the *beis midrash*.

---

2 Reported by Yechezkel Shraga Frankel.

One of the Rebbe's followers, Yechezkel Friedman, related that when he was a youngster he once hid in the *beis midrash* to see how the Rebbe conducted himself. "I came to the *beis medrash* as the Rebbe was davening *maariv*, totally absorbed in his prayers. I hid in a corner to see what he would do. The *beis midrash* emptied, and he sat learning Gemara out loud, hour after hour until sometime after midnight. Then he stopped learning and for almost an hour recited the bedtime Shema with great intensity and concentration. At last, he took a bench into the small room he had off the *beis midrash*, lay down on it, and went to sleep. A few short hours later I heard the Rebbe's voice reciting *Birchos HaTorah*. A new day had begun."

When he davened, his prayers sent chills through his listeners' bodies. His supplications to the Almighty were punctuated by cries and groans, yet he stood before his Creator ablaze in his love for Him. He davened this way both on weekdays and on Shabbos.

Often when he recited the blessing of *Ahavah Rabbah* he would repeat each word two or three times, tears streaming down his cheeks like a child pleading to his father. Sometimes he would change the words, choked with emotion, reciting first, "Enlighten our eyes to Your Torah, attach our hearts to Your commandments" and then, "Enlighten our eyes to Your commandments, attach our hearts to Your Torah." Then he threw himself on the ground in entreaty and humility.

Faith in the Almighty and Dedication to His Yeshivah

The Rebbe's faith in God was unyielding. One Sukkos night, a fire broke out in the communal sukkah, which shared a wall with the Rebbe's private sukkah. The Rebbe's followers immediately ran into his sukkah and implored him to leave. The Rebbe said calmly, "I am wearing the coat of the Bnei Yissaschar and the *gartel* of another holy tzaddik. I am not afraid of the fire at all." Amazingly, the fire destroyed the entire community sukkah except for the wall which adjoined the Rebbe's sukkah.[3]

The hallmark of the Rebbe's years in Klausenberg were his efforts in teaching Torah. Soon after he arrived, he established a yeshivah in which many exceptional students studied. He himself would teach them for several hours a day.

One of his students, Reb Yirmiyah Yisraeli, recalled, "There were about one hundred students in the Klausenberg yeshivah. We would eat in a different community member's home each day, and the Rebbe himself made sure that not a single student was lacking. His devotion to us was like that of a father to his children. He would feed several students in his own house, where there was sometimes not enough food to go around. The Rebbe would give the students his own portion and then spend the rest of the day in an absolutely joyous mood, even though he hadn't eaten a thing."

The Rebbe's Fame Spreads

Revered by his community, the Rebbe became well known throughout the area. Many great rabbinic and chassidic figures came to visit Klausenberg, including two sons of the Divrei Chaim, Rabbi Shalom Eliezer of Raczfert and Rabbi Yeshayah of Czekov. Another frequent visitor was Rabbi Avraham Yehoshua Frind, who served as the rabbi of Nasad and authored the *sefer*

---

3 Reported by Pinchas Zelig Berger in the book *Mazla Tava.*

Maor Yehoshua. The Rebbe was extremely close with him and they conferred regularly on many issues, including various ways of easing the burden of the Jewish community. The Rebbe also developed a very close relationship with the great Hungarian Torah scholar Rabbi Shaul Brach, the rabbi of Kashoi.

In 1937, the Rebbe was offered a position on the *beis din* of Rabbi Yosef Tzvi Dushinsky in Jerusalem. The idea of settling in the Holy Land and assuming a prominent position in Jerusalem was very appealing to the Rebbe. Yet he hesitated before accepting the position, recalling the experience of a certain Rabbi Yosef Leib Kahana who went to the Divrei Chaim to receive a blessing as he prepared to make aliyah. Before he had a chance to say a word, the Divrei Chaim said to him, "Reb Yosef Leib, do you think that only in the Holy Land you can attain perfection? If a Jew sanctifies his own four cubits of halachah, then everywhere he goes is like Eretz Yisrael for him."[4]

Uncertain what to do, the Rebbe wrote to his mother in Rudnick for advice. She responded that in her opinion he should stay for the time being in Klausenberg, since he was still too young to assume the position in Jerusalem.[5]

Interestingly, many years later, during a *shiur* in Bnei Brak, the Rebbe related that before the Holocaust he had wanted to move to Eretz Yisrael and tried to obtain a visa, but was unable to because of objections raised by the British Consul and the interference of irreligious Zionist activists.[6]

---

4 Quoted in *Shefa Chaim, Yehi Ohr*, p. 18, and other places.
5 Reported by Nesanel Wax.
6 Reported by Yehoshua Heller.

Chapter 2

The Early Years of the War

The Lord Is My Rock

When World War II broke out in September 1939, the Klausenberger Rebbe was thirty-five years old, a leader of the Klausenberg community, happily married, and blessed with eleven beautiful children. The outbreak of the war opened before him an abyss of darkness and loss. It had been decreed from Heaven that he should be tested with terrible suffering and tragedies, more than the ordinary mortal can withstand. Yet the Rebbe clung to his faith in the Savior, the God of Yaakov. Just like David HaMelech, about whom it says, "And David became stronger in Hashem, his God" (*Shmuel* I 30:6), all of the Klausenberger Rebbe's strength came from the fact that Hashem was his God. He did not require anything more than that.

At the end of the Holocaust, when the Rebbe learned that not a single member of his family had survived, his response was, "I have lost everything. But I have not lost Hashem."[1] The words of the *Chovos HaLevavos* were fixed on his lips: "My God, You have starved me and left me all alone and placed me in dark

---

1 Reported by Yehoshua Veitzenblum.

places, and in Your might and greatness I have sworn. Even if I shall be burned in a fire I shall not stop loving You and rejoicing in You" (*Shaar Ahavas Hashem*, ch. 1).

Behold, Days Are Coming

The Holocaust did not come as a surprise to the Rebbe. In mid-1939, when he was invited by the Jewish community of Bilgoraj, Poland, to spend a Shabbos there, he delivered a pointed rebuke over the spiritual decline of the generation. He spoke of the need for both men and women to be more vigilant and observant of the laws of modesty and warned of the terrible decrees that were likely to come.[2]

Some five years later, on Rosh Chodesh Cheshvan 1944, the Rebbe ascended the *bimah* in the *beis midrash* in Klienwardein, the community where his family had found refuge during World War I, to speak to the Jews of that community and beseech them to repent. In a thunderous voice he warned of the dangerous and grave situation. "The Jews of Poland have already been destroyed. Who knows what is in store for us?" He repeated the warnings that he had given to the Jews of Bilgoraj five years before.[3]

Hunted Down on Their Own Streets

In the first few years of the war, when Polish and Lithuanian Jews were already being destroyed by the millions, the Jews of Romania and Hungary were still living a relatively normal existence. Even during these four years, however, there were prob-

---

2 See note above.
3 See note above.

lems and persecutions day in and day out. The fierce anti-Semitism and hatred took on such extreme proportions that every Jew felt that his life was imperiled.

In the summer of 1940, after the Vienna Accords were executed, Transylvania was divided into three countries: Czechoslovakia, which was placed under Nazi German rule as a so-called "protectorate," Romania, and Hungary. The city of Klausenberg, which had been the capitol of Transylvania, was thereafter ruled by the Magyars, who were Nazi collaborators.

Out of concern for the welfare of his Jewish brethren, the Rebbe followed all the political developments carefully. He kept a map of Europe on his desk which he marked with the changes that resulted from the German advance and the new borders.

When the Hungarian army entered the Klausenberg area at the end of the summer of 1940, the Jews were overcome with fear. Yosef Yom Tov Vizel, a resident of Klausenberg, recalled, "The Hungarian soldiers and police immediately began to oppress the community and particularly the Jews. We were afraid to leave our houses. Just crossing the street meant taking your life in your hands if you were Jewish.

"I once met the Rebbe at the *mikveh* on a Shabbos morning. We began to walk home together. On the way, we encountered a group of Hungarian soldiers armed with revolvers standing and talking in the street. When they saw us, the soldiers began to whisper among themselves, exchanging smirks and meaningful looks that made their intentions obvious. I was totally panicked. I thought quickly to myself, *How can we escape from their line of vision?* But out of great respect for the Rebbe I did not dare to do anything. I just continued walking with him.

"As was his way, the Rebbe walked slowly with his eyes practically shut. But just as we came near the group of soldiers, he opened his eyes wide and stared at them. He recited chassidic sayings and words of faith to assure me that I should have no fear because Hashem protects His servants. I barely understood a word he said because I was so terrified. But the Rebbe kept talking to me. He spoke loudly as though he wanted the others to hear. And then, lo and behold, a miracle occurred. We passed our enemies without incident. They were intimidated by the Rebbe's holy presence and did not dare touch us."

My Flesh Will Dwell Securely

Yosef Yom Tov also related the following incident from that period. "Like many other Jews, shortly after the Hungarians came in, I was drafted into the *munka-tabor*, a forced labor troop. I was very worried about what the future would bring. We knew that the world was being engulfed in flames, and I felt the need to cry my heart out to someone who would listen. I went to the Klausenberger Rebbe and told him of my worries, asking him to bless me that I should live.

"The Rebbe lovingly grasped my shoulders and blessed me. He quoted the verse, '*Af besari yishkon lavetach* — even my flesh will dwell securely,' and said, '*Besari* stands for your name, Yosef Yom Tov *ben* Sarah Rivkah.'

"As it turned out, that was the last time that I saw the Rebbe during the war years. Many things happened to each of us. With Hashem's great kindness we both survived by way of miracle after miracle. Many years later, in 1955, when the Klausenberger Rebbe came to Eretz Yisrael for the first time, I went to greet him in Yerushalayim, bringing my young son, who was born after the Holocaust. I said to the Rebbe, 'Here, you see, your prayer and blessing were accepted. *Af besari yishkon lavetach.*'

"The Klausenberger Rebbe nodded his head in agreement. Remembering every detail of that incident, he told me how happy he was."

Another survivor from the Rebbe's community, Eliezer Shtissel, told the following story: "I was taken from Klausenberg by the Hungarians and interned in a forced labor camp. I came to the Rebbe to bid farewell and to ask that he bless me that I should remain alive. The Rebbe instructed me to observe the following three practices strictly so that I would be spared: 1) to be very careful to keep my head covered; 2) to observe the laws of washing one's hands; and 3) whenever I was in danger to say to myself, 'The mother of Avraham was Amatlei bas Karnebo,' '*Yavo hamelech veHaman hayom* — the King and Haman should come today' [the first letter of each word spells Hashem's name], and '*Elokah deRebbe Meir aneni* — God of Meir, answer me.' As he stretched out his hand to say good-bye, he said, 'If you will observe these three things the Almighty will watch over you and you will be saved.' And that is exactly what happened."

Remaining Strong in the Face of Hardship

In later years, the Rebbe would occasionally speak of the events of those times. During a Shabbos HaGadol *derashah* in 1980, he mentioned, "In Hungary during the Second World War, there was a tremendous food shortage. Some rabbis [in other cities] permitted the use of *kitniyos* during Pesach because of the difficult situation. But there was not a single Jew in

Klausenberg who followed that leniency. They withstood the difficulties with great dedication and devotion."[4]

On another occasion the Rebbe related, "During the first days of World War II, the government sent police to every shul in Klausenberg to protect the Jews on Shabbos and holidays. They came to our *beis midrash*, as well. On Simchas Torah, when they saw the Jews dancing enthusiastically in honor of the Torah from morning to night, they stood bewildered and amazed. At night a policeman came up to me and said, 'I do not understand. These people are dancing all day without drinking even a drop of liquor? How is that possible?' He simply could not understand that one could dance without being drunk, for every 'holiday' of his ended with hundreds of people being killed and injured."[5]

Decrees and Expulsions

In 1941, after the Hungarian army joined the German offensive against Russia, the persecution of Hungarian Jews became even greater. All kinds of false pretexts were employed to persecute the Jews.

One of these pretexts was the enactment of the Law of the Examination of Hungarian Citizenship, which required all Jews in Hungary to prove that their families had lived within the borders of the country since 1851 and were included on the tax rolls as taxpayers. Anyone who could not establish these two facts was subject to deportation to Galicia, where his fate would be the same as that of the thousands of Jews already under Nazi

---

4 *Imros Tzaddikim*, p. 157.
5 Quoted in *Yahadus* (Tammuz 1971), p. 7.

rule. Tens of thousands of Hungarian Jews were caught in this cruel trap and turned over to the Gestapo by the local police or simply killed by Hungarian soldiers in the forests near the border.

Because the Klausenberger Rebbe was born in Rudnick, Galicia, he was officially considered a Polish citizen. Thus, his days in Hungary were numbered. One day a squad of Hungarian soldiers came to his house with an official government order to take the Rebbe and his family to a central location in the capital city of Budapest where all the deportees were being assembled. The soldiers brutally ordered the Rebbe and his family be ready to leave in ten minutes.

The Rebbe accepted this decree quietly and calmly, without any signs of concern. He took his tallis and tefillin and three *sefarim* which he was in the midst of studying. The Rebbetzin and children quickly gathered some food and clothing and were ready to leave at the appointed time. They were soon loaded into a Hungarian army vehicle for the journey to Budapest.[6]

Imprisoned

In Budapest they were separated. The Rebbe was jailed separately with other VIPs who were going to be transported by the Nazis across the border. This group was eventually sent directly to the crematoria in Auschwitz. The Rebbetzin and the children were taken to a temporary lockup for foreigners, near Budapest, until their fate was determined.

Close friends and community activists in Klausenberg went into immediate action to rescue the family. They contacted the

---

6 Reported by Yosef Yom Tov Vizel.

Agency for the Protection of Rights of Hungarian Jewry, which was composed of religious as well as irreligious Jews, and after a concerted effort succeeded in convincing the heads of the agency to intercede on the Rebbe's behalf. Fortunately, their efforts were successful. After several days the Rebbe was released and transferred to the camp for deportees where his wife and children were imprisoned.

The Klausenberger Rebbe later recalled his incarceration in this camp. "I myself was for a time in the International *Lagar* which was like a small international ghetto. There were many nationalities there, French, Ukrainians, Slovaks, and so on. They all received food packages which meant the difference between life and, God forbid, death. But we Jews did not get anything at all."[7]

The Rebbe's followers and the leaders of the Klausenberg and Budapest communities persisted in their efforts to have the Rebbe freed. After several weeks their efforts paid off. The Rebbe and his family were finally released and returned home to Klausenberg.[8]

The Faithful Shepherd

Even though it was clear that life was not going to get any easier for the Jews in Klausenberg, the Rebbe refused to leave his followers and made absolutely no effort to save himself from the terrible plight there. Instead, he opened his home to the Jewish refugees who streamed into Klausenberg, escaping from the advancing German army. The Rebbe did this knowing full well

---

7 Quoted in *HaModia* (Hebrew edition), Jerusalem, *Erev Shavuos* 1984.
8 Reported by Yitzchak Berger, a Jew from Klausenberg who survived the war.

that by helping these illegal refugees stay in Klausenberg, he was putting himself in danger.

One of the refugees, a brilliant yeshivah student from Slabodka by the name of Rosenberg, became an adopted member of the Rebbe's family. He and the Rebbe's oldest son, Lipele, became close friends and study partners. By divine providence this young man was present one day when the Rebbe's second son, Chaim Hirsch, buried several precious manuscripts and religious objects that the Rebbe had inherited from his ancestors. Among the buried items were original writings of the Bnei Yissaschar, the shofar which the Rebbe used on the high holidays, pages of original handwritten Torah insights of the Divrei Chaim and of his son Rabbi Baruch of Gorlitz, and an ancient letter written by the Kabbalist Rabbi Shmuel Vital.

This young man miraculously survived and after the Holocaust endangered his life to return to Klausenberg to recover the buried items. He found all the items untouched and returned them to the Rebbe.[9]

The Fate of the Rebbe's Family

The Rebbe's mother and siblings in Poland faced far graver danger than the Rebbe did in Hungary. Several weeks after the outbreak of the war, the Rebbe learned that his mother had managed to flee Rudnick in a horse-drawn wagon, together with her son Reb Avraham and other members of her household. They made it to Kreshov and from there to the Russian border.

---

9 Related in the introduction to *Chiddushei Mahartza LeHilchos Chanukah* by Rabbi Tzvi Elimelech of Dinov (New York, 1954).

Five days later the Nazis stormed Rudnick and murdered the Jews of the city.

For a time, the Rebbe's mother lived in the Galician town of Berezon and then under very difficult conditions in Lvov. The Rebbe managed to keep in contact with her and to send her small food packages. But one day in 1941 the news came that the Nazis had entered the city of Lvov and had massacred thousands of Jews there, among them the Rebbe's saintly mother, Rebbetzin Chaya Mindel.

To Lighten the Burden of the Jewish People

Very little by way of documented facts is known about the Rebbe's life between 1941 and the Nazi conquest in 1944, though from that which is known an extraordinary picture emerges. Even during those mad days of terror the Rebbe never stopped studying Torah and davening and pleading on behalf of the Jewish people. He completely forgot about himself and was only concerned with the plight of his brethren. Knowing what lay ahead, he tried with all his might to lighten the burdens of his tortured brothers by elevating them to higher worlds.

Shalom Eliyahu Pelberbaum, who lived in Klausenberg at that time, related that one Shabbos afternoon he noticed that the Rebbe was only pretending to eat the food he was served. After some careful investigation it became clear to him that the Rebbe was fasting. The previous night, the Rebbe had seen visions of terrible future events. Since one is required to fast upon hearing such news, even on Shabbos, the Rebbe fasted. To avoid frightening his community, though, the Rebbe conducted his regular *tisch* with the usual melodies and Torah discourse as if nothing had happened.

Shalom Pelberbaum also spent his last Purim in Klausenberg with the Rebbe, about a week and a half before the Nazi invasion. With heavy hearts the Jews of Klausenberg gathered together with their Rebbe, knowing that the situation was very grave. One leader of the community, Yosef Chaim Rothschild, could bear the situation no longer. Weeping bitterly, he burst out, "Rebbe, how will we be able to carry on? You must beseech the Almighty to have mercy on the Jewish people."

The Rebbe did not utter a word. Instead he let out a piercing wail. It was a cry that shook everyone who heard it.

Sukkos in Raczfert

Before Sukkos of 1943, the Klausenberger Rebbe went to the local botanical garden in the hope of finding the four species. After a long search he found a small palm tree on which after some difficulty he was able to identify a branch which could serve as a kosher *lulav*. But when he tried to obtain permission to cut it, the official in charge demanded in payment a large sum of money, so large that the Rebbe was not able to pay it.[10]

The Rebbe decided to spend *yom tov* with his great-uncle (and his wife's grandfather) Reb Shalom Eliezer in Raczfert, having heard that his uncle had obtained the four species. He took his eldest son, Lipele, with him, and they remained in Raczfert for the entire *yom tov*.

That year, because of the state of emergency, only three *esrogim* could be found in all of Hungary. One was in Raczfert in

10 Reported by Shalom Eliyahu Pelberbaum.

the possession of Reb Shalom Eliezer; the second was in the city of Grossvarden in the possession of the Moznitz Rebbe, the author of the *Imrei Chaim*; and the third was obtained by the leaders of the Budapest Jewish community for the Belzer Rebbe, who was then living in Budapest. Many important rabbis and chassidic Rebbes came to Raczfert that year to perform the mitzvah of the four species.

The Klausenberger Rebbe stood out among all these great rabbis and holy men. Because of his great love for his great-nephew, Reb Shalom Eliezer sat the Klausenberger next to him at his *tisches* and accorded his great-nephew with the respect due royalty. He also asked him to read the Torah portions in shul, an honor usually reserved for Reb Shalom Eliezer himself. The huge congregation that had assembled in Raczfert listened attentively and was greatly uplifted by the Klausenberger's unique reading of the Torah.[11]

Thousands were drawn to the Rebbe wherever he went. Young people, who had heard so much about the Klausenberger's awesome diligence in Torah study, took shifts to follow his every movement and see when he slept. When he davened, people gathered around him to listen, even though he tried to pray out of public view. His prayers touched the hearts of all who heard them and motivated them to repent.[12]

Several great Torah scholars who were in Raczfert for *yom tov*, Rabbi Meir Yosef Rubin of Kerestier, Rabbi Mendele Korader, the *dayan* of Miskolc, and Rabbi Yisrael Ephraim Fishel Rota, the rabbi of Veiditchka, engaged in heated Torah

---

11 Reported by Chaim Alter Rota.
12 Reported by Yehoshua Veitzenblum.

discourses with the Rebbe. Challenging and debating each other throughout the night, they resembled the scholars of old.

Reb Yisrael Ephraim Fishel of Veiditchka was so impressed that when he returned home during Chol HaMoed, he told another rabbi who was on his way to Raczfert, "Be sure not to miss the opportunity to take a *kvittel* to the holy Klausenberger Rebbe. He has become a truly great man."[13]

The Prayers of a Tzaddik

The Rebbe's great-uncle Reb Shalom Eliezer did his utmost to save the Jewish people from the decree of destruction that had been sealed by the Almighty. On the last Rosh HaShanah, right before the blowing of the shofar, he cried out, "I see harsh judgments and a terrible divine apathy. Let us recite together the psalm 'My God, My God, Why Have You Forsaken Me?' "

On Yom Kippur during the recitation of *U'Nesaneh Tokef*, Reb Shalom Eliezer made a subtle change in the text of the traditional prayer. Instead of saying, "You will open the Book of Chronicles and it will be read [*u'mei'alav yikarei*]," Reb Shalom Eliezer wept, "*U'mei'alav yikara* — and it will tear itself!"

Understanding the gravity of the Jews' situation, the Klausenberger sought to defend his people to Reb Shalom Eliezer that Sukkos. Their words could be heard on high and perhaps they would find merit for the Jewish people. "Every single Jew, even if all he does is recite the Shema, is worthy of being saved from all bad," he told his uncle.

Reb Shalom Eliezer agreed. "The great Sage Rabbi Shimon bar Yochai said so."

---

13 Reported by Chaim Alter Rota, the son of Reb Yisrael Ephraim Fishel.

The Klausenberger said, "You must be referring to the statement of Rabbi Shimon bar Yochai in the Talmud that 'The Almighty said to the Jewish people, "Even if you have not observed the mitzvos except for reciting the Shema in the morning and evening, you will not be handed over to [your enemies]" ' (*Sotah* 42a)."

Reb Shalom Eliezer nodded his head in agreement.[14]

In Sanctification of God's Name

That Sukkos was the last holiday celebrated by the Sanzer chassidim of Hungary. At the end of the winter of 1944, the Nazis invaded Hungary. Several months later, on the last day of Pesach, they rounded up the Jews of Raczfert and transported them to nearby Nirdhaus. Reb Shalom Eliezer was taken together with his immediate family and his grandchildren, including his great-grandson Lipele, the Klausenberger Rebbe's eldest son, who had been visiting Raczfert for *yom tov*. Many desperate attempts were made to try to save Reb Shalom Eliezer, but he refused to leave his community, saying, "I dwell among my people."

After a few short weeks this saintly man was sent along with many others to the crematoria in Auschwitz. In his last moments he asked for water to wash his hands, a yarmulke to wear on his head, and tzitzis to clothe himself. On Wednesday, 17 Sivan, 1944 (5704), he was murdered *al kiddush haShem*.

---

14 The Rebbe related this conversation in a Chumash class, *Parashas Emor* 1977.

Chapter 3

The Enemy Pounces

The Nazi Conquest of Hungary

On Sunday, March 19, 1944, Hitler's brutal storm troopers invaded Hungary and seized the country in a raging fury. Hungary was the last European country which still had a large concentration of Jews, approximately one million in number. These Jews now saw with their own eyes the sword of destruction dangling over their heads. The objective of the Nazis was well known: to kill every Jew, young or old, man or woman.

Time was beginning to work against the Nazis. The Soviet army had already begun its counteroffensive, regaining control of the Ukraine as it advanced on the Carpathian Mountains. The bloodthirsty Nazis worried, with good reason, about their impending defeat, yet they pursued relentlessly their primary goal of the destruction of the Jewish people.

Under the command of the chief butcher Adolph Eichmann, they pounced on their prey with viciousness and single-minded determination. They issued decrees, established ghettos, and began sending transports of Jews to Auschwitz. The recently built gas chambers enabled them to murder over ten thousand Jews every day.

The Klausenberger Rebbe in Hiding

When the SS entered Klausenberg and took charge of the city, the Rebbe was concerned that he would be taken captive, since it was well known that the Nazis always began their torture with the spiritual leaders of a community. The Rebbe therefore slipped out of his house and hid for several weeks in an open grave in a cemetery on the outskirts of the town.

Although he had enough food with him to remain in the cemetery for some time, the Rebbe did not feel safe there. Worried that his hiding place might become known to others, the Rebbe secretly approached a man named Yirmiyah Tessler, who owned a beverage factory, and asked if he could hide in one of the underground storage bunkers on Yirmiyah's property.

The Rebbe used to go to the Tessler house every year to recite *Tashlich*, since the home was situated on the banks of the nearby river. When the Rebbe finished his prayers, he would rest for a few minutes in the Tessler house. Before he left he would wish Yirmiyah a "*g'mar chasimah tovah.*" Now the situation had changed completely, and the Rebbe had to seek a place of refuge on the Tesslers' property.

Yirmiyah immediately agreed to the Rebbe's request, suggesting also that since he did not have Hungarian citizenship papers it might be better for him to obtain a fake passport and travel to Banya. There he would be a stranger and would be able to get placed in a forced work detail or travel to Romania, just thirty minutes away. In an attempt to relax the Rebbe, Yirmiyah made light of the negative reports that Klausenberg was hearing. The Rebbe, however, refused to relax, understanding that they were standing at the threshold of a terrible tragedy, the like of which had never occurred before.

Seeing the logic in Yirmiyah's suggestion, the Rebbe asked him, as a community leader, to provide for his family, who would remain in Klausenberg. (Two of his children had already left Klausenberg: Lipele was in Raczfert and Chaim Hirsch was with other relatives.) The Rebbe asked that Yirmiyah find a place for them to hide, since, lacking Hungarian citizenship, they were in danger of being transported out of Hungary.[1]

The Four Questions

The Tessler family immediately took the Rebbe's remaining nine children into their home. Klausenberg had been placed under curfew, its residents only permitted to leave their homes a few hours each day. Yirmiyah Tessler's description of the time is as follows: "We were cloistered in our homes in fear of what would happen in the coming hours and days. The gate of our house was locked. No one came in and no one went out. Whenever we heard the sound of footsteps or the doorbell ringing, our hearts began to beat rapidly. We thought to ourselves, *Maybe these are the footsteps of the enemy, coming to attack us.* We would hide in the attic until we knew for sure that the danger had passed."[2]

The night of the seder that year was particularly dark and depressing. The bitter herbs brought home to the Tesslers the

---

1 Reported by Yirmiyah Tessler in *Zechor V'Al Tishkach* (Jerusalem, 1968), p. 56ff.

2 Ibid., p. 16.

very real bitterness of their daily lives. The Rebbe's fifth son, Meir'l, captured everyone's feelings with a few short words when he rose to ask the *Mah Nishtanah*. The little boy began, "Dear Reb Yirmiyah, I would like to ask you the four questions." Suddenly he stopped and sighed.

One of the Tessler girls asked, "Meir'l, why did you sigh?"

"Because of the troubles that are about to befall the Jewish people," Meir'l answered.

"I Can't Give Up My Daughters"

Several weeks before this incident, on the Rebbe's last Shabbos in Klausenberg, the Rebbe was approached by a simple Jew, one of his followers. The man told the Rebbe that his non-Jewish neighbor had offered to hide his three daughters until after the war ended. Although this man understood what was in store for him, he was determined not to give his daughters to this non-Jew for safekeeping. Better that they not survive than that they leave their faith and live as non-Jews.

In later years the Rebbe related, "I tried in vain to convince him that it was better that he agree to his neighbor's idea. Even if, *chas veshalom*, he would not return, it was not at all certain that his daughters would give up their faith. They were already intelligent teenagers who would be able to withstand the pressures and remain Jewish. The man, however, would not change his mind.

"He answered, 'Rebbe, I will obey everything that you tell me to do except this! I will not be able to die at peace if I know that perhaps, God forbid, my daughters will be forced to convert and assimilate.' "[3]

---

3 Quoted in *Yahadus*, Shevat 1973, p. 4.

In the Nadi-Banya Labor Camp

In Iyar 1944, the Rebbe reached the city of Banya (also called Nadi-Banya) and was conscripted into forced labor. The Banya camp held some five thousand Jews who had been transported there for labor by the Hungarian army.

Yitzchak Berger of Klausenberg, another Jewish prisoner in Banya, recalled, "We lived in relatively decent conditions, under the circumstances. The most difficult aspects of our lives was the forced labor and the painful fact that we had been completely separated from our families. The camp was surrounded by high barbed wire fences, but it did have an exit into the forest through which non-Jews would come and sell us as much bread and milk as we wanted. Thus, we did not suffer from hunger."

One of the camp authorities was a Hungarian captain who concerned himself with helping the Jews and saved many lives. This captain protected the Klausenberger Rebbe and many other prisoners for as long as he could.[4]

On at least one occasion, the Rebbe was given a furlough to leave the camp for Shabbos. The Rebbe spent this Shabbos with one of his followers who lived in the city. He conducted a *shalosh seudos* in the Chassidish *beis midrash* of the city. As they were singing *zemiros*, the Rebbe's eyes filled with tears. Spreading his hands heavenward, he pleaded, "Master of the Universe, I beg You, have mercy on us!"[5]

The Rebbe had an extraordinary impact on the Jews in the labor camp and those in the local ghetto. Many of the wealthy Jews in the ghetto were interrogated and tortured by the police

---

4 Tessler, p. 58.
5 Reported by Tzvi Moskowitz.

to reveal where they had hidden their money. When they could no longer withstand the torture, some asked the police to allow them to seek advice. They made their way to the Klausenberger Rebbe to ask what to do. In most cases, the Rebbe advised them not to disclose their hiding places because the Nazis could not be trusted to keep their word and would likely kill them anyway. This was exactly what happened. Even those who did disclose where their money was hidden were sent to their deaths in Auschwitz.[6]

In later years, the Rebbe related how he personally witnessed the evil character of non-Jews and their intense hatred for the Jewish people: "When I was in Banya during the war, the local non-Jewish population learned that all the Jews of the city were going to be transported to Auschwitz in just a few days. They entered the ghetto and cruelly asked the Jews — their former neighbors — to leave their possessions for them, saying, 'You are going to be killed anyway — why not give us your valuables?' Because of their 'long-standing friendship,' they wanted to take everything from them while they were still alive!"[7]

Difficult Days

One Vizhnitzer chassid named Ben Tzion Tabak recalled, "I remember the Klausenberger Rebbe very well from those terrible days in the Banya camp. Because of the Nazis' orders the Rebbe was forced to completely shave his beard. His appearance was very depressing, but his eyes resembled fiery coals. He con-

6 Reported by Yaakov Edelstein the Israeli journalists' yearbook (1960), p. 216.
7 From a Chumash *shiur, Parashas Shelach,* 1979.

stantly encouraged his fellow prisoners with words of faith and *chizzuk*. On Shabbos I davened in the Rebbe's private minyan. He prayed with such intensity and devotion. At *minchah* on Friday afternoon, during the chazzan's repetition of *Shemoneh Esrei*, he cried bitterly during the recitation of *Atah Chonen*, 'You Endow Man with Knowledge,' and *Hashiveinu Avinu Lesorasecha*, 'Return Us, Our Father, to Your Torah.'

"One day we were all ordered to line up outside in rows. Then the soldiers conducted a cruel and merciless search for hidden money and valuables, searching each prisoner's entire body indiscriminately, rummaging through every pocket and exploring everything he had in his possession. When they did not find anything, they pounced on us in a great rage.

"Finding our tefillin, they tore them open, brutally yanked out the sacred scrolls inside, and threw them on the ground with great contempt. Then they looked through the insides of the tefillin. When they found nothing, they returned the empty *batim* to us.

"I was a young man then, and I was bewildered and frightened by the spectacle, unable to believe my eyes. But the Rebbe remained calm and gently reassured me. After I picked up my tefillin scrolls and the Rebbe's, the Rebbe asked me to go to the camp kitchen and ask one of the butchers for some *gidim*, animal sinews, with which he could sew the *batim* closed again. [According to halachah, tefillin *batim* must be closed with sinew.] He told me that even sinews from nonkosher animals would be acceptable, as long as they were sinews.

"I went to the kitchen, where, to my great surprise, I was given the sinews. In a short time, I was able to bring them to the

Rebbe. The Rebbe immediately went into the barracks and laid the sinews out on his mattress to dry them out. After checking the scrolls carefully, he got a needle and sewed the two sets of tefillin closed again. We rejoiced together, the great Rebbe and little me, as if we had found a great treasure."

The Last Day in Banya

Yitzchak Berger related what occurred on the Rebbe's final day in the Banya camp. "I was not able to see the Rebbe every day because he was busy with thousands of prisoners. But I did see him on our last day in the camp.

"The camp authorities woke us up for roll call at four o'clock that morning. We were forced to stand in rows and brutally searched to make sure that none of us would take anything of value with us when transported to the concentration camps. The search lasted for close to fifteen hours. We were forced to stand the entire time, the sun beating down on our heads. We were hungry, thirsty, and worn out, broken and exhausted from all the humiliation and the beatings we had endured. By evening we could hardly remember our own names.

"Only the Klausenberger Rebbe did not lose his focus. When he saw the shadows were growing longer and the search had not yet ended, he whispered to those standing near him that they should put on tefillin if they could do so without being detected by the Nazis. He urged his neighbors to pass the message on, and quickly, because the sun would soon set."

A River of Blood

When the search was over, the thousands of prisoners were

transported by cattle car over the Polish border to the death camp known as Auschwitz.

At the exact same time, the Jews of Klausenberg were being sent in mass numbers to their deaths in the gas chambers of Auschwitz. The Rebbetzin and the children who were with her were on the fifth transport from the Klausenberg ghetto. They were murdered on June 2, 1944[8] (11 Sivan, 5704). The saintly Rebbetzin Pessel died *al kiddush haShem* and ascended to the heavens with her pure children. In a single moment in time, she established nine sacred altars to the Almighty.

The Rebbe later said about his children, "They had very holy souls. Their mother did not even cross the street with them frequently, lest, *chas veshalom*, they be hurt by an evil eye."[9] He mourned their loss deeply and cried bitterly after the war when *Parashas Vayishlach* was read. This parashah narrates the story of our forefather Yaakov's efforts to protect his household and his eleven children from his brother, Esav. The verse states, "He took them and crossed the river." The Rebbe said, "I, too, took my household and eleven children across a river; they crossed a river of blood along with multitudes of pure and holy Jews."[10]

---

8 Tessler, p. 51.
9 Reported by Yehoshua Veitzenblum.
10 Reported by Yehoshua Heller.

Chapter 4

On the Edge of the Abyss

The Valley of Death

Auschwitz was the largest of the concentration and death camps that the Nazis built throughout Europe. There were almost no survivors from this valley of death; the masses of inmates were tortured viciously and forced into backbreaking labor to their last breath. The camp's smokestacks worked overtime as its gas chambers and crematoria, built specifically to exterminate vast numbers of people as quickly as possible, carried out their jobs. Close to two million Jews met their tragic deaths at Auschwitz.

Terror ruled the prisoners of Auschwitz. Beneath the smoke that spewed forth nonstop from the crematoria, man, the greatest of God's creations, was pulverized by men who behaved like the lowest of beasts. Bloodthirsty and cruel, the Nazi camp authority trampled its victims with an uncontrollable and insatiable rage. There is not enough ink nor any words that can adequately describe the very real nightmare that was Auschwitz.

In a World of His Own

The Klausenberger Rebbe was transported to Auschwitz

along with thousands of other persecuted Jews being sent to their deaths. The Master of the Universe, however, had decided that he should live, and thus he was selected for work by the infamous Nazi butcher, Dr. Joseph Mengele. Saved from the gas chamber, the Rebbe was sentenced to a life worse than death. Yet it was here that the Rebbe was elevated to great and lofty levels of service of God, publicly sanctifying his Creator's name with every action.

The Rebbe's incredibly saintly behavior during his imprisonment in Auschwitz and other concentration camps was an amazing thing to behold, almost beyond the comprehension of an ordinary mortal. The Rebbe lived in his own world. Although he was physically in the world around him, mentally and spiritually he was completely separate from it. Auschwitz has been called a planet unto itself in a different universe. The lives of people there were unlike the lives of people anywhere else in the world. Yet the Klausenberger Rebbe managed to create for himself in the midst of the horrors a planet within a planet. While most of the Auschwitz inmates thought only of basic survival, the Rebbe's thoughts were focused on much loftier matters.

In the concentration camps the Nazis conducted an inhumane program of persecution and degradation that broke the inmates' spirits and brought out their most animalistic instincts. The prisoners fantasized about getting a piece of dry bread or an edible potato peel in order to satisfy their terrible hunger. But the Rebbe was concerned only with his spiritual needs. He wanted to put on tefillin, to wash his hands properly, to pray, and to bless the new moon.

Most inmates could think of nothing but their own tortured

existence. The Klausenberger Rebbe ached for the Almighty who was suffering along with His people, as the verse says, "For I am with you in times of trouble."

When things were particularly difficult and the prisoners lay on the floor utterly hopeless, bleeding from numerous wounds, the Klausenberger Rebbe could be heard murmuring, "From Your place, our King, You will appear and reign over us, for we await You...." and "When will You reign in Zion?"[1]

The Rebbe's needs and concerns were completely unlike those of his fellow prisoners. When most prisoners finally got a piece of longed-for bread, they would gulp it down immediately. The Rebbe, however, would stand there on Shabbos, famished, with the bread in his hand and try to decide how best to please the Almighty. Should he eat it so as not to fast on Shabbos and make Kiddush over the bread? Or should he not eat since he lacked water with which to wash his hands?[2]

One survivor, Rabbi Avraham Yaakov Kish, recalled that he once met the Rebbe in a death camp. The Rebbe did not talk about what was happening in the camp; rather, he discussed Torah thoughts and ideas. He shared with Avraham Yaakov an idea on the first verse of *Parashas Chukas*, "This is the statute of the Torah that God has commanded you to say." Hidden in this verse, the Rebbe explained, are three keys to Torah study: 1) One should review his studies 101 times (hinted to in the word *tzivah*, which has a numerical value of 101). 2) When a person learns Torah he should envision the Almighty standing before

---

1 Reported by Rabbi Shmuel Unsdorfer, who heard it from the Rebbe's barracks mates in Auschwitz.

2 Reported by Chaim Alter Rota.

him (hinted to by the word *God*). 3) A person should study out loud (hinted to in *to say*).

"If you do these three things," said the Rebbe, "you will not forget the Torah which you study."[3]

He Is Always with Us

Wherever the Rebbe went, he clearly felt Hashem's presence accompanying him. Upon entry into Auschwitz, confronted by the brutal German soldiers with their disparaging curses and vicious beatings, the Rebbe encouraged his fellow Jews, "Do not be frightened! HaKadosh Baruch Hu is present even in this place. He has preceded us here, and He is waiting to save us. There is no place in the world where HaKadosh Baruch Hu is not present."[4]

Seeing three young yeshivah students who had arrived in the camp on his transport, the Rebbe walked over to them and began encouraging them to take strength in their faith in the Almighty. With great emotion, he asked them, "Do you believe that the Creator is here with us?"

The boys answered, "Yes, we do."

The emotion in his voice rising, the Rebbe said with great emphasis, "Remember, the Ribbono shel Olam is here with us. He will redeem us. In the merit of your *emunah* you will be saved and will live to leave this place." All three young boys did indeed survive the war.[5]

A short time later, when a despondent inmate cried out in

---

3 Quoted in *Mazla Tava*, p. 42.
4 Reported by Chaim Alter Rota.
5 Reported in the *Sanz* newspaper, issue 266, p. 35, as heard from Wolf Straheli, one of the three boys.

agony, "We are all going to die here!" the Rebbe told him, "You have no right to say such a thing about me. I am certain that you and I will both be saved. If you do not believe that, you may say what you want about yourself, but do not say such things about me."

"How do you know that we will be saved, Rebbe?" asked the man.

The Rebbe answered, "HaKadosh Baruch Hu is here with us, and He will certainly rescue us."[6]

The Rebbe lived through Auschwitz with the verse "Though I shall walk in the valley of death I shall not fear, for You are with me" (*Tehillim* 23:4). He fulfilled the teaching of the Sages, "Even when a sharp sword is lying on one's neck, he should not despair of mercy" (*Berachos* 10a). No matter what befell the Rebbe, he never stopped believing in and clinging to the Almighty.[7]

The Rebbe once found several torn pages covered with Hebrew letters in the garbage between the barracks in Auschwitz. He bent down to retrieve the pages and saw that they came from *Pirkei Avos*. The Rebbe hurriedly gathered up the torn pages with trembling hands and kissed them with deep emotion. Later, the inmates secretly gathered around the Rebbe in a corner of the barracks to satisfy their spiritual thirst with the life-giving elixir of *Pirkei Avos*.[8]

Determined to Serve His Creator

Even during the most terrible times, the Rebbe never lost

---

6 Related by the Rebbe during a lecture on *Parashas Vayishlach*, 1984.
7 Reported by Rabbi Mordechai Chaim Slonim, who heard it from the Rebbe.
8 Reported by Auschwitz survivors in the *Sanz* newspaper, issue 266, p. 36.

his focus on *avodas Hashem*. Right under the noses of the Nazis, he studied Torah, davened, and observed the mitzvos. Without regard for his personal safety, he avoided the most minor transgression of Torah law.

A survivor named Asher Brenner recalled, "In Auschwitz I was placed in the same group as the Klausenberger Rebbe. The Rebbe suffered even more than the rest of us because of his stubbornness. He refused to eat nonkosher food. He had managed to bring his tefillin into the camp with him, and he put them on every day. Notwithstanding the great danger, he organized daily minyanim for prayer services. We often forgot about Shabbos completely, but the Rebbe avoided desecrating Shabbos every week and made sure that no one else did the work that was imposed on him.

"All this, of course, drew the attention of the *Kapo*s, and they punished the Rebbe with vicious beatings. (The Rebbe accepted the beatings calmly, whispering to himself, 'For God is righteous and I have rebelled against his words' or 'May it be Your will that my death be my atonement.' He also sometimes murmured, 'Because you have not served Hashem with joy.') But slowly a change in attitude took place among the *Kapo*s. Looking at him with new respect, they started to treat him more kindly. They finally came to recognize the Rebbe's unique character, principles and total devotion to Hashem."[9]

Later in the Rebbe's life, he told one of his followers, "In Auschwitz I wore only a torn, thin garment, even in the bitter cold. I preferred it to the other rags we were given because the buttons were sewn on the left in the custom of my holy ancestors. Who knows — perhaps because I was so careful about what

9 Yehoshua Eibschitz, *BeKdushah U'BeGvurah* (Tel Aviv, 1976), p. 230.

I wore I was allowed to live."[10]

On another occasion, overcome by emotion, the Rebbe related, "When I was imprisoned by the Nazis, I walked around in wooden shoes. One day I found a shoe padded with a piece of leather. When I lifted it up to look at it, I saw that the leather was really a piece of parchment from a tefillin scroll. It read: 'Be very careful lest your hearts be seduced.' I began to cry over the desecration of the holy tefillin and over the message that had been sent to me from Heaven."[11]

In Honor of Shabbos

On Shabbos afternoon, the Rebbe would go from barracks to barracks and beg his fellow inmates for a bit of onion so that he could fulfill the custom of his ancestors to eat an onion in honor of Shabbos. His eyes lit up when someone gave him a few edible scraps of onion that had miraculously been obtained from the camp kitchen. Who but the Klausenberger, in the midst of this hell, had no other worries except finding an onion for Shabbos?[12]

The Rebbe never failed to say words of Torah to himself on Shabbos, particularly in the late afternoon, at the time of *seudah shelishis*. Covering his head with the bottom of his shirt or with the thin blanket from his bunk, he would recite words of Torah to himself.[13]

An irreligious Jew was once standing near the Rebbe and overheard him explaining the verse from *Tehillim*, "Sing to God

---

10 Reported by Yehoshua Veitzenblum.
11 Related in a speech given on Chanukah 1976.
12 Reported by Pesach Langsam.
13 Reported by Moshe Weiss.

a new song for He has performed amazing feats. His right hand and holy arm have helped Him." The Rebbe translated the verse into Yiddish and then gave an explanation.

"I did not understand what he was saying," recalled the man, "but the verse enraged me. Where were God's amazing feats? Where was His outstretched arm? Many years and life experiences later, however, I recalled the explanation that the Klausenberger Rebbe had given and the idea entered my mind, *Wasn't that in and of itself an amazing feat? In the hell of Auschwitz there was a Jew who was still faithful to the Almighty and took strength in the amazing feats that He had promised to perform in the future.* This thought caused me, late in my life, to begin to return to our faith."[14]

Years after the Holocaust, the Rebbe's followers noted that the Rebbe never failed to expound on the Torah at *seudah shelishis*, even when he was alone and no one else could hear him. Once they asked the Rebbe the significance of saying words of Torah at that particular time. He gave a short and mysterious reply: "The Torah must be expressed in this world; it has a purpose...."[15]

A Sign from Above

When the Rebbe reached Auschwitz, he took pains to tell his fellow prisoners that according to halachah they were required to preserve their health and they had to eat whatever they were given. "Since our enemy's intention is to destroy both our bodies and our souls, it is a mitzvah for us to do the opposite

---

14 Reported by Rabbi Shmuel Unsdorfer, who heard it from an Auschwitz survivor.
15 Eibschitz, p. 230.

and preserve ourselves. Now is not the time to refrain from eating and endanger one's life."[16]

Despite this firm ruling for his fellow inmates, the Rebbe himself refused to eat *treif*. He was determined not to defile his mouth with any morsel that was not kosher, no matter what the consequence.

When the Rebbe's fellow inmates noticed this and began asking how he could endanger his own health, the Rebbe would not answer them. When they threatened that if the Rebbe did not eat the food from the camp kitchen they would also stop eating it, the Rebbe became concerned. He asked them to give him some time to think about it.[17]

The Rebbe later related the amazing event that took place which served for him as a sign that Heaven approved of his decision not to eat any nonkosher food.

"I reached Auschwitz on an *erev Shabbos* at about 10:00 in the morning. As soon as we entered the camp, a meat breakfast was served to those who had been selected for work. Everyone pushed to get some. My fellow Jews encouraged me to come and take some food, but I told them that under no circumstances was I going to eat nonkosher food from the *reshaim* who had taken everything from me. I fasted all that *erev Shabbos*. By evening I was very hungry and weak.

"On the next day, Shabbos Kodesh, I again heard the announcement for breakfast. Again I did not go. When the barracks emptied and I was left alone, I burst out crying. Although I had undertaken to accept everything that happened to me with

16 Reported by Avraham Eidels.
17 Related in *Mazla Tava*, p. 42.

love, that afternoon, I sobbed bitterly. 'Master of the Universe, I have been left with nothing. You have taken everything from me. My family is gone; I am left barefoot. And now I should eat nonkosher food? I don't want to eat *treif*!"

"As I sat there sobbing, a Jew entered the barracks and walked up to me. 'Are you the rabbi from Klausenberg?' he asked. The question frightened me, for the murderers made it a practice of sending rabbis and spiritual leaders to the gas chambers first.

"Another Jew came over just then and said, 'You must come immediately. There is someone waiting for you by the door.'

"I had no choice but to go to the doorway, even though I was afraid that a *Kapo* or an SS officer would be waiting there.

"At the door I saw an older man, a Jew. He asked me, 'Was the Kishinov Rebbe your uncle?'

"I was stunned. How did this man know about me here in Auschwitz? 'Yes, he was my uncle,' I answered.

"Quickly he gave me a loaf of bread and a small jar of jelly. 'I brought you something to eat so that you can satisfy your hunger.'

"In an instant, he vanished. I never ever saw him again.

"I saw clearly then that there is indeed a God in this world. My decision not to eat *treif* had been validated not only for me but also for all my fellow prisoners, who had been pressuring me to eat the camp food. At that moment, I again took upon myself not to eat *treif* food, no matter what would happen, particularly since HaKadosh Baruch Hu Himself had provided me with what to eat. I made Kiddush on the loaf of bread and sat down to eat my Shabbos meal.

"During the entire year that I was imprisoned by the Nazis,

yemach shemam, I did not eat any nonkosher food, nor did I desecrate Shabbos. And I was protected by heaven. Not a single *rasha* knew who I was. Several times I was literally just a step away from death, and I saw firsthand that HaKadosh Baruch Hu protects those who observe His mitzvos and study his Torah. The merit of my ancestors protected me.[18]

In the beginning, the Rebbe decided he would drink plain milk, as long as nothing had been mixed into it, even though it hadn't been milked under the supervision of a Jew. Later he changed his mind and stopped drinking this milk. This change of heart resulted one time when his stomach swelled, a symptom of starvation. The Rebbe heard those near him whispering that his end was near. Immediately, he said to himself, *If I am going to die anyway, why should I drink milk that was not watched by a Jew?* He stopped drinking the milk. Several days later, the Rebbe's health returned and the swelling of his stomach disappeared.[19]

One of the Rebbe's fellow inmates recalled how the Rebbe would not even take a sip of coffee from the camp kitchen, except on very rare occasions when he was assured that the water had been heated in a special cauldron and that a Jew had added some coals to the fire under the cauldron so that it would not be *bishul akum.*[20]

Later in life, the Rebbe publicly thanked the Almighty for watching over him during those days of wrath and for enabling him to observe the laws of kashrus and avoid eating any food that had even the remotest possibility of being prohibited. He managed to survive without eating anything that was cooked in the oven of a

18 Related in a Chumash *shiur, Parashas Re'eh,* 1984.
19 Reported by Avraham Eidels.
20 Reported by Moshe Weiss.

non-Jew and without eating *chametz* on Pesach. "I can testify about myself that my mind was not warped through the ingestion of forbidden foods, for I was always careful about this."[21]

The Jewish People Will Survive

In the second volume of *Shefa Chaim*, the Rebbe relates, "Once, in the concentration camp, a professor asked me sarcastically, 'What do you have to say now about the destiny of the Jewish people?'

" 'It will be good,' I answered. Seeing that he was surprised by my answer, I explained. 'Although I am not a prophet, I know in my heart that my prediction is correct. The same way that I know that day will follow night, I know that we will survive. If you ask me about my personal fate, I can't answer...but I know for certain that the Jewish people are destined to be saved. Our evil oppressors will be destroyed completely.

" 'This point has been proven many times in the history of our people,' I continued. 'Numerous enemies have risen against us and attacked us mercilessly, but in the end none of them have remained in existence. Complete nations have been erased from the face of the earth, but the Jewish people remains!

" 'There are many Jewish families which take great pride from the fact that someone, many generations before, gave his life *al kiddush haShem*. But no one considers it a source of pride to have a murderer in the family.'

"When I was finished, the professor admitted, 'You are right.' "[22]

---

21 Related in a Chumash *shiur, Parashas Shelach*, 1979.
22 *Shefa Chaim*, vol. 2, p. 205.

Chapter 5

In the Warsaw Ghetto

Warsaw after the Ghetto Uprising

After the failed Warsaw Ghetto uprising during Pesach of 1943, the Nazis liquidated the ghetto, destroying what was left of the largest Jewish community in Europe. Warsaw had been left *Judenrien* (devoid of Jews). A year later, the Nazis decided to bring a group of concentration camp inmates to the city to collect the valuables left in the ghetto and demolish the ruins so that the bricks and steel could be sold to Polish contractors. Some thirty thousand Hungarian Jews were chosen for this task, since they would not be able to converse with the local population.

Among the Hungarian Jews chosen to go to Warsaw was the Klausenberger Rebbe. After several months in Auschwitz, the Rebbe was found fit for hard labor in Warsaw and was transported by cattle car to the bombed-out ghetto.

In the Warsaw Ghetto Ruins

After three days of traveling with no food or water, the prisoners arrived in Warsaw. There they were housed in two concentration camps which had been prepared for them, one in the Jewish cemetery on Gensha Street and the other at the outskirts of the city in the suburb of Praga. In these camps, the inmates were divided into groups of two thousand people, with each group housed in a separate barracks. They left the barracks each morning to work in the city from sunrise to sunset under the constant surveillance of the SS.

For the first time the Hungarian Jews were able to fully comprehend the extent of the atrocities perpetrated by the Nazis in Warsaw. Warsaw was not simply a deserted city; it was a destroyed city, piled high with skeletons and mounds of ashes. The great city of Warsaw, the pride of European Jewry, was in ruins. Not a building remained intact.

Clearing the ruins was both difficult and dangerous. The Jewish prisoners were forced to dig under the foundations of the bombed-out buildings, tie ropes to the walls, and pull on the ropes until the walls crumbled and fell. Sometimes the falling walls collapsed on the Jewish laborers and buried them alive. Often as they cleared out the ruins, the laborers found basements and bunkers full of bodies of Jews who had been shot or gassed, or who had succumbed to hunger and disease.

A Shot to the Soul

One hair-raising sight after the other met the eyes of the Jewish laborers. One of the hardest ones to bear was in the ruins of a bombed-out *beis midrash*. While the Rebbe and his group were working, a bulldozer drew out from under the mounds of ash and bricks several ripped sections of a desecrated Torah scroll.

The Rebbe turned ashen and collapsed in a faint. His fellow

laborers rushed over and splashed water on his face to revive him. It was only with great difficulty that they succeeded. The tragedy of a desecrated Torah scroll shook the Rebbe more than anything else, like Eili HaKohen, who when informed of the defeat of the Jews in the hands of the Philistines and of the death of his two sons in battle nonetheless remained strong. It was only when he was informed that the holy ark had been captured that he collapsed and died.

Alexander Kratz, one of the survivors, recalled, "The sight of the desecrated Torah scroll struck each of us in our hearts. Some of the prisoners started to cry. But the Klausenberger Rebbe was the only one who actually fainted. We all saw clearly how deeply he was affected. It was as if he had been stabbed in the heart."[1]

Spiritual Needs over Physical Needs

Moshe Eliezer Einhorn, a survivor from the forced labor detail who was in a barracks adjoining the Rebbe's, had the opportunity to closely observe the Rebbe during those days. He related the following story:

From time to time, the prisoners found hidden coins, gold, and other valuables among the ruins, which they traded secretly with the local Poles for a potato or a piece of bread. Many of the prisoners suffered from typhoid because of the inhumane and unsanitary living conditions in the barracks. Thus, every prisoner was on the lookout for something which would protect him from the disease.

---

1 Reported by Alexander's son Tzvi Kratz, who also worked in the Warsaw Ghetto.

One prisoner was cleaning out a bombed-out factory when he discovered a large sum of money. Taking the treasure, he secretly contacted a Pole and arranged to buy loaves of bread and liquor on a regular basis. The man then offered some of his bread and liquor to the Rebbe, begging him to eat so that he would have some strength. The Rebbe refused the offer, asking instead for something that he needed for his spiritual needs — two challah loaves for Shabbos.

The Rebbe's Tefillin

The Rebbe still had a pair of tefillin in his possession in Warsaw. With great determination, he had succeeded in hiding it from the Nazis even during the many body searches he had undergone. Early each morning before they were sent to work, some three hundred Jewish prisoners would wait in line to don the Rebbe's tefillin. Time was so limited that the Rebbe did not have a chance to recite the Shema while wearing his tefillin, yet he wanted to enable as many men as possible to fulfill the mitzvah of tefillin.[2]

One survivor, Eliyahu Yaakov Steinmetz, remembered the unforgettable experience of waiting in the "tefillin line" in the Rebbe's barracks in the Warsaw Ghetto. The Rebbe, he recalled, davened almost all day, with tears running down his face, while he worked in the ghetto ruins. Some of his fellow prisoners kept a close watch on him while he was absorbed in his prayers, lest a guard approach.

From time to time the Rebbe would organize a minyan at great personal danger. The Jews who knew of the Rebbe and his

2 Reported by Moshe Eliezer Einhorn.

manner of prayer from home would gather around him when he prayed. Others, who were witnessing it for the first time, gawked in amazement. In the midst of his prayers the Rebbe would talk to the Almighty in Yiddish like a child speaking to his parent. In the ruins of the Warsaw Ghetto he davened exactly as he had in his own *beis midrash* in Klausenberg.[3]

One young man, Aharon Yehoshua Nussenzweig, who lived two barracks away fr' ·n the Klausenberger, was told in confidence one day that t .ere was a pair of tefillin in the Rebbe's possession. Secretly, he rushed to the Rebbe's barracks and expressed his desire to fulfill the mitzvah of tefillin. Smiling, the Rebbe gladly gave him the set of tefillin. The young man put them on eagerly. He was not able to return every day, but when he had another chance to go he hurried over to the Rebbe's barracks. This time, however, the Rebbe sadly gave him only the *tefillin shel yad*. The Nazis had confiscated his *shel rosh*.

One day, a devoted follower of the Rebbe, Menachem Mendel Weider, was walking to work among the ruins of the Warsaw Ghetto and found a pair of crushed tefillin that had survived the bombing. He quickly brought them to the Rebbe. Immediately, the Rebbe hid them in his barracks and kept their existence a secret so that they would not fall into Nazi hands again. Only five or six Jews were let in on the secret and were permitted to put them on when there was no danger of being discovered.

When the men could put the tefillin on during the day, they were as happy as could be. But many times they were not able to evade the guards and they had to wait for night to come. Under the cover of darkness, they donned the tefillin without a

---

3 Reported by Yaakov Kahn.

berachah and quickly recited the first section of Shema. The Rebbe put the tefillin on last and would wear them for longer than the rest.[4]

Heavenly Protection

The entire time in the Warsaw Ghetto the Rebbe's diet consisted of only dry bread and unpurified water. Occasionally, someone would find him a small onion or a morsel of tasteless food.[5] The Rebbe became very weak, but he was determined not to bend. In his weak state, he could hardly work and was in danger of being removed from the labor force and sent off to share the fate of other infirm and elderly Jews. The Rebbe, however, enjoyed a special heavenly protection.

Mendel Weider related, "In the beginning, the Rebbe was forced to carry building materials — large bricks, both whole and broken. The work was nearly impossible for him. I was full of pity for him because I knew that if the guards saw that he was not fit for the work they would exterminate him immediately. I always tried to stay at his side so that I could carry things for him, using many tricks to hide the truth from the guards.

"Later on, the Rebbe was ordered to demolish what was left of a destroyed wall of a house with hammers and other such tools. He was too weak to bend over for long periods of time to do the job. I fashioned a long handle for the hammer for the Rebbe to use, at least when the guards were passing by.

"Throughout the work day, the Rebbe wept bitterly. As he cried, he whispered over and over, 'Why should the nations of

4 Reported by Menachem Mendel Weider.
5 Reported by Eliyahu Yaakov Steinmetz.

the world say, "Where is your God?" ' I was amazed that the
Rebbe was not crying over his own trials and tribulations, but,
rather, over the desecration of God's Name that was taking
place."

The Rebbe's Refusal to Shave

Mendel also related the following story: All the Warsaw
Ghetto laborers were ordered to shave their beards. Anyone who
refused to comply was likely to be killed. Despite the danger, the
Rebbe refused to shave his beard with a razor. His devoted followers tried to find a scissors or a shaver for him since these are
permitted in halachah, but they were unsuccessful. The Rebbe
therefore wrapped his beard and face in a handkerchief as if he
had a toothache, so as not to be caught.

A few weeks later, the Germans discovered that some Jews
had escaped from the ghetto by hiding in the wagons carrying
out the ghetto valuables. In order to prevent this from happening again, they issued a new order: All prisoners were forced to
shave a narrow strip of their scalp once a week. That way they
would be easily identified outside of the ghetto, even from afar.
A shaver was brought to the camp for this purpose, and Mendel
would "borrow" it occasionally from the designated barber and
bring it to the Rebbe.

Before this was accomplished, the handkerchief wrapped
around the Rebbe's face once saved him from a beating. As mentioned above, the Rebbe cried all day as he worked. One day, a
particularly cruel supervisor approached the Rebbe and began
screaming at him. Waving his fist in the Rebbe's face, he yelled,
"Why are you crying?" Thinking quickly, Mendel hurried over

and explained that the Rebbe was suffering terribly from a toothache, as was plain to see from the handkerchief wrapped around his face. "The pain is so great," he said, "that he can't help crying like a baby."

Mercifully, the guard accepted the explanation and left the Rebbe alone.

The Chosen People

The following story was related by the Rebbe himself on many occasions: "One day, when we were standing on the top of a building, a sudden rainstorm came up. Despite the driving rain and gusts of wind, the Nazis ordered us to continue working and finish our jobs. The work was practically beyond human ability.

"One prisoner could take it no longer. Turning to me, he screamed, 'Are you still so happy that you are a member of the Chosen People?'

"I answered, 'From now on when I say the words, "*Atah vechartanu*, You have chosen us from all the nations," I will concentrate even more than before, and I will rejoice without limit. But for the fact that HaKadosh Baruch Hu chose us from all the nations, I too would have become an oppressor like these. Better that I remain in my current state of oppression than that I become, *chas veshalom*, like one of them. How fortunate I am!' "

Who Is Like Your People, Israel

The Rebbe also told of the following incident: One of the workers in the Warsaw Ghetto was a Lithuanian Jew who was an expert locksmith. Because his expertise was needed by the SS, he was given more freedom and better meals than the average prisoner. One day, this Jew snuck into the Rebbe's barracks to seek the Rebbe's advice about a halachic issue.

"In my capacity as a locksmith," he began, "I am forced to work on Shabbos, and I end up transgressing Torah prohibitions every single Shabbos. I would prefer to switch to carrying heavy loads because then I will only be violating a Rabbinical prohibition on Shabbos."

The Rebbe asked, "How do you plan on being switched?"

The man explained, "I will burn my hands so that I will not be able to work with locks anymore." He stood confidently in front of the Rebbe, awaiting an answer.

Most of the people in work details that involved carrying heavy loads collapsed within a few days from the unbearable labor. The Rebbe therefore told the man, "I don't advise you to do that. You shouldn't put yourself in such danger."

The man would not be deterred. "I do not want to transgress so many Torah prohibitions!"

Only with great difficulty was the Rebbe able to convince him that in his present job he was in a position to help many Jews and save them from starving to death, and thus he should not worry about the Shabbos desecration involved.[6]

The Plight of an Assimilated Jew

In 1983, while speaking to the students of Beis Chana in Williamsburg, the Rebbe told, in detail, the following personal experience:

---

6 Related in a compilation of the Rebbe's talks edited by Rabbi Yaakov Glick.

"In the camps, we were forced to sleep on the floor. Forty-two people were stuffed into a small room, and within two weeks only I and one other person were left alive. The other forty had died from starvation and disease. This other man, who came from Budapest, and I slept on the ground, enveloped in darkness and surrounded by insects and rodents.

" 'Are you Jewish?' I asked my companion.

" 'Of course! Why else would I be here?' he answered.

" 'Who are you?' I probed.

" 'I am the president of the National Bank of Hungary.' This was the most important finance position in Hungary; it meant that this man's picture appeared on all Hungarian currency.

"I asked again, 'Are you Jewish?'

"This time he answered, 'No.'

" 'Didn't you just say that you were?' I queried in surprise.

"The man quickly explained himself: 'I converted to Christianity!' Clearly he had abandoned the faith of his ancestors in order to move up society's ladder.

"It was impossible to fall asleep, so I continued the conversation, gazing pityingly at him. 'Are you married?'

" 'Yes, but my wife is a Christian,' he answered.

" 'And she did not join you here?' I asked with mild astonishment.

"Angrily, the man responded, 'How could you even think of such a thing? Why should she have come here? To suffer as much as I am?'

"Innocently, I responded, 'I do not understand. Doesn't a good, devoted wife follow her husband wherever he goes, even to Gehinnom if necessary? Would a good wife leave her husband alone in this state?' Without pausing for breath, I continued, 'Tell me, did you live well?'

" 'What kind of a question is that? In the thirty years we lived together, I bought her the best of everything. I gave her all the good in the world!'

" 'If so, I am really shocked,' I said. 'How is it possible that you treated your wife so well for thirty years, and she is only willing to share the good times with you? In hard times like this, she leaves you to deal with it alone?'

"We stopped talking then. The night passed and in the morning we were called to work again. The next night, I struck up a conversation again. 'Tell me, did you accomplish important things for the Hungarian government?'

" 'Certainly,' the former banker responded. 'When I was hired to manage the National Bank, the economy was very depressed. The forint's value had gone way down. With one thousand forints you could hardly buy anything. I made it into a real currency, a strong currency. Hungary became prosperous, thanks to my hard work, and it began to trade with the whole world. I accomplished great things in the fields of finance and business. You never heard of me?'

"I shrugged my shoulders apologetically. 'I am not involved in such matters. I am not a businessman or a banker.'

"The banker asked in surprise, 'You really mean you don't know who I am and what I was? To this very day you won't find a single gentile in Hungary who doesn't recognize my name.'

" 'Then how is it that you were sent here, and the Hungarian nation did not protest? After all, you did so much for them. How could a person as important and as accomplished as you be run out of the country and into a concentration camp without any legitimate reason?'

" 'Why are you provoking me so much?' the banker exploded. 'Perhaps you can tell me why you are imprisoned here?'

" 'I am just a poor rabbi,' I answered. 'I never did anything for a gentile. I never even gave one of them a glass of water. They hate me. But you did so many good things for them. How can they hate you? I would expect them to carry you on their shoulders, not send you to a concentration camp.'

" 'Well, as you can see they did not carry me on their shoulders.'

" 'I simply cannot understand it. After all, you converted to Catholicism and became a complete non-Jew in order to be like them and to be accepted by them — and they ignored it all.' As an aside, I asked, 'What about your children? What do they do?'

" 'My children? One is a doctor, the other a lawyer, and the third a successful businessman.'

" 'Did you also provide for them?'

" 'Of course!' the banker answered. 'I sent them to the best schools so that they would be well educated.'

" 'And why did your children not come after you?' I pressed. 'Even when a person dies his children follow the casket to the cemetery. Your children have left you to be exiled in shame.... They didn't follow you to the border. Not a single one has come here to see where their father is and what is happening to him.'

" 'You are hurting me very much with your words. You want to annoy me.'

" 'I don't want to annoy you, God forbid. I just want to understand how bitter your situation is.'

"We continued talking until late at night. My words began to penetrate the assimilated banker, for on the third night, he initiated the conversation. 'You know, Rabbi, I've been thinking about your words all day.... I have come to the conclusion that you are right!' He expressed genuine regret for having converted, for having married a non-Jewish woman, and even for spoiling his children so much. The banker saw clearly that absolutely nothing from his pathetic life remained with him. 'I made a mistake,' he cried in a choked voice. 'I made a terrible mistake with my life.'

"On the fourth night, the banker was no longer among the living. I was grateful for the opportunity that had been sent my way. For wherever he was, he had at least done *teshuvah* and regretted his deeds a day before his death."[7]

In the Line of Fire

In his later years, the Rebbe related the following incident: One day the Zunder Commandos from Lublin (a liquidation unit of the German army) arrived in Warsaw. Their uniform buttons proudly displayed skulls, and it was rumored that wherever they went they never left a living prisoner. The news spread throughout the camp that they were about to move the prisoners to a central location in Warsaw where they would all be killed by the Nazis. The Zunder Commandos soon began to prepare the prisoners for that, but with the Almighty's great mercy, the heads of the *Wehrmacht* did not agree to the plan and the prisoners were saved.

About two weeks later, word went out that the Command was again getting ready to move the prisoners from the camp. At

7 Quoted in the Yiddish paper *Shalsheles Beis Sanz* (Brooklyn, 1995), p. 121ff.

that point, several prisoners in the Warsaw Ghetto made contact with the local partisans and began planning an uprising. The plan was complicated, though, and the planners had several unresolved issues. Unable to reach a consensus, they decided to ask the Klausenberger Rebbe for advice.

One of the prisoners went to the Rebbe and outlined the escape plan. They were going to try to storm the gates of the camp and run away. Although they knew that many prisoners would likely die, perhaps some would be saved. The man asked if the Rebbe thought it made sense to proceed in this manner.

The Rebbe was perplexed. The question was a difficult and serious one, and he did not have any *sefarim* to consult with. Before long, however, he ruled: "Until we see that the Nazis are about to exterminate us, it is prohibited for anyone to sacrifice his life and put himself in a situation of certain death. But one must remain vigilant, and as soon as it becomes clear that the Nazis, *yemach shemam*, are ready to attack us, we must do everything in our power to rise up against them."

Until the crisis passed, the Rebbe tried to encourage the inmates, telling them that HaKadosh Baruch Hu would surely take them out of Warsaw.[8] The prisoners accepted this advice and broke off their contact with the partisans. Some time after, when the majority of the prisoners had been transported from Warsaw, the Rebbe among them, the five hundred remaining prisoners tried to execute an uprising and mounted an assault. The Nazis mounted a counterattack and ultimately killed every single Jew in the uprising.[9]

8 The Rebbe related this story on November 30, 1982, in Bnei Brak.
9 Tessler, p. 60.

A Failed Escape Attempt

With the Red Army counteroffensive near the Polish border in the summer of 1944, the prisoners began to have renewed hope that they would survive. One day, when the Russian artillery could be heard near Warsaw and shells and bombs fell occasionally in the city, the prisoners were sure that their guards would take cover in the bomb shelters and bunkers. Perhaps, they thought, this would be an opportune time to escape.

However, the danger in an escape was great. The inmates knew that the Poles had been promised five kilograms of sugar for every live Jew that they turned over to the Germans, and Poles waited outside the ghetto walls to catch escaping Jews. Nonetheless, the prisoners decided to try to escape, and the Rebbe participated in the attempt. A large group of prisoners crawled on all fours right up to the walls of the ghetto. But, contrary to their expectations, the guards had remained on their posts and opened fire upon seeing them. After several inmates were injured, the prisoners were forced to give up and crawl back.[10]

When the Russian bombing increased, the Rebbe told the Jews around him, "This is a good sign. There is no doubt in my heart that we will be saved and the *reshaim* will not succeed with their wicked plans."[11]

Avinu Malkeinu

The Rebbe's encouragement heartened his fellow prisoners on many occasions. Aharon Yehoshua Nussenzweig recalled: "On one particularly horrific day, the SS awoke before sunrise to

10 Reported by Mendel Weider.
11 Reported by Eliyahu Steinmetz.

conduct a 'selection.' They had decided to thin the ranks of the camp's population by exterminating inmates who were no longer needed. We were ordered to line up in neat rows to have our fates decided.

"To this day I can see before me that frightful picture. We stood there bewildered and terrified, the angel of death upon us. It was still quite dark and a cold wind whipped our faces. The SS officers ran excitedly between the rows, energized with a sudden and peculiar murderous spirit, screaming orders left and right.

"I was gripped with fear, feeling that everything was lost, and I could not stay in my place in line. When the guards were looking in the other direction, I slipped out of my line and began wandering from row to row, searching for a life preserver.

"Finally I hit upon an extraordinary scene. It was the Klausenberger Rebbe pouring out his soul in quiet prayer. He was surrounded by the rest of the Jews in his group, gripped by the fear of death, also praying silently. Although his sobs were muffled to avoid attracting the Nazis' attention, the Rebbe cried and groaned bitterly without letup.

"I came closer. The Rebbe was reciting the prayer of *Avinu Malkeinu*, and with every sentence he uttered those around him responded in kind. 'Our Father, our King, tear up our evil decree.... Our Father, our King, avenge before our eyes the spilled blood of Your servants.... Our Father, our King, act for the sake of Your abundant compassion.... Our Father, our King, thwart the counsel of our enemies....'

"The cries of the Rebbe broke my heart. The Nazi murderers were running around like wild, bloodthirsty animals, arbitrarily selecting who would live and who would die, while the group of Jews came closer to the Klausenberger like sheep flocking to their shepherd.

"The Rebbe's cries rose to the heavens. When the selection was concluded, we knew for sure that Hashem had willed for us to remain alive."

A Close Brush with Death

Several days later, when it became clear to the Germans that they would not be able to withstand the Russian offensive, they decided to finish off the temporary camp in the Warsaw Ghetto. The prisoners, who had been working for several months among the ruins of the ghetto were taken to a field outside of Warsaw. The Klausenberger Rebbe was among the group.

The feeling was ominous; the ghetto workers knew their end was near. When they reached the field, escorted by the armed SS guards, they saw freshly dug ditches in front of them. They were commanded to strip their clothes off and walk up to the ditches. A group of soldiers aimed their machine guns at close range.

A step away from death's door, the prisoners did as they were told. The silence was broken by the choked cries of *Vidui* and *Shema Yisrael*. Some prisoners eagerly awaited the moment that their misery would finally come to an end.

Suddenly, from out of nowhere a fancy vehicle drove up at high speed. To everyone's shock, it came to a screeching halt at the edge of the ditches. A high ranking officer jumped out and screamed, "Halt! Halt!" The SS officers stared at him. "I just received via telephone a special order from the head of the SS in

Berlin," the officer announced. "He said to delay the execution because the Dachau concentration camp needs laborers. These prisoners must be sent there as quickly as possible."

The prisoners had been saved, once again, from death! The Rebbe's life was spared again in this miraculous event.[12]

The silence was broken by a command, "Get dressed!" The Nazis quickly began organizing the prisoners for the trip to Dachau, located in Germany.

The Journey to Dachau

The march to Dachau began two weeks before the Poles began a revolt against the Germans in Warsaw. On Friday, the eighth day of Av, July 28, 1944, the inmates left Warsaw and began a journey of such incredible torture that it is impossible to comprehend.

For most of the prisoners, the journey to Dachau was not to be a normal trip, but, rather, a journey to a certain death, conducted in the cruelest manner imaginable. Forced to move at high speed until their strength was exhausted, the downtrodden inmates suffered terribly at the hands of their sadistic guards. Thousands of Jews died during the march.

The Klausenberger Rebbe miraculously reached Dachau alive after two weeks, one of a mere two thousand Jewish souls who survived the journey.

---

12 Reported by Mendel Weider.

Chapter 6

The Death March

Violence and Horror

There are no words to describe the cruelties perpetrated against the six thousand downtrodden Jews, the Klausenberger Rebbe among them, during the march from Warsaw to Dachau. They were forced to cover seventy miles on foot, not walking like normal people, but in a mad sprint during which the brutal SS soldiers lashed at them with whips and steel poles to make them run faster and faster — as if they were a herd of animals.

The march was conducted under conditions of intense heat, starvation, and dreadful thirst. Half-crazed by the frequent beatings and inhumane torture, the prisoners were not allowed to stop, even for a moment, to rest or relieve themselves. As it says in *Megillas Eichah*, "They walked on without strength before the pursuer."

Those who could not keep up were shot to death. Those lucky enough to find a puddle of dirty water by the roadside bent down quickly to lick some up before the guards saw them. A prisoner who ripped a leaf or two off a tree branch and sucked it to quench his terrible thirst, if only for a brief moment, was considered lucky.

After marching on foot for days, the persecuted Jews made a significant part of the journey by train. Crammed into cattle cars, they were forced to stand day and night without moving, under completely inhumane conditions. Many died en route.

Through it all, the Rebbe experienced countless incidents of divine providence and lifted the spirits of those around him.

Leaving Warsaw

Before the prisoners left the Warsaw Ghetto area, they were given some dry bread and salty cheese to take with them. The camp commander announced that any prisoner who felt too weak or tired to make the trip by foot should tell the guards immediately so that he could be assured a place on a bus. About 240 prisoners were fooled by this announcement. They were shot to death before the march began.[1]

Fortunately, the Klausenberger Rebbe was not among them.

The prisoners left the ghetto and began their march. Outside the ghetto walls, life went on as usual. The Poles went about freely. Store shelves were fully stocked with all kinds of food — bread, rolls, and even white bread. There were so many grocery products on the shelves that there was no need for customers to hoard food. Down these same streets marched nearly six thousand starved, exhausted Jews, wondering if they were the last Jews in Europe.

On the upper stories of the buildings, blinds and windows were

---

1 Reported by Aryeh Lida in *Sefer Sosnowitz*, vol. 2 (Tel Aviv, 1974), p. 208.

opened. Poles stared out curiously at the Jewish prisoners, whose wooden-soled shoes filled the streets with noise. A few looked on with teary eyes, but most reacted with pleasure at the sight. Gleefully, they screamed at the prisoners, "*Zhidi, kati* (Jews, cats)!"[2]

As they left the city the marchers were directed onto the main road, on a route of some twenty-one miles, the distance established by the Germans for each day of the march. After eating the terribly salty food which the Nazis had given them, they became extremely thirsty, but there was no water to drink. The hot summer sun beat down on them, and the dust kicked up by six thousand pairs of legs parched them further.

The commander of the march and his assistants rode in cars and on bikes in the rear to make sure there were no stragglers. Those who did not keep pace were run over and then shot to death by the soldiers who marched alongside the prisoners, taking turns so as not to get tired.[3]

When some non-Jewish farmers tried to give the prisoners pails of water, they were brutally attacked by the SS guards, who chased them away and spilled the water on the ground. In the afternoon, the group reached a river. The Nazis told the prisoners that they could go and drink, but when the first group approached the river, they let their attack dogs loose and opened fire. The prisoners could see the river, but they could not drink any water. At night, they slept in an open field surrounded by armed SS guards.[4]

---

2 K. Charmatz, *Kashmaren* (Brazil, 1975).
3 Reported by Meir Shraga Perdelsky in *Sefer Sosnowitz*.
4 Reported by Perdelsky and Lida in *Sefer Sosnowitz*.

Shabbos Chazon

That night was Friday night, the ninth of Av, Shabbos Chazon (the fast of Tishah B'Av would be observed on Sunday). Before the war, on a Shabbos of the ninth of Av, the Rebbe would recall the words of the Rebbe of Apta in *Ohev Yisrael*: "Shabbos Chazon is greater than all other Shabbosos of the year, especially when it coincides with Tishah B'Av which falls on Shabbos." He would rejoice with the *Shechinah*, which feels no pain on Shabbos. This Shabbos Chazon, however, was very different.

Early on Shabbos morning, a piercing shriek aroused the inmates from their sleep. With the instincts of hunted animals, they rose quickly to avoid the beatings of the *Kapos* and SS guards, who screamed at them to hurry and stand up for their morning lineup. The Nazis counted the rows of prisoners and distributed to each one a small piece of bread and some dirty water, and then the morning's march began. They were forced to assume a very fast pace to make the most of the early morning hours, before the sun reached its height.

Every so often a loud command was heard: "Run! Run!" The prisoners ran with the last of their strength, their thin bundles on their backs. The Rebbe, however, refused to carry his bundle because it was Shabbos. He looked for a way to dispose of it without endangering himself. Next to the Rebbe marched one of his followers, Reb Yaakov Friedman. Without asking any questions, he grabbed the Rebbe's bundle and said, "It is better for one man to carry than for two."

A guard spotted the exchange. In a flash, he was upon the Rebbe, striking him angrily with the butt of his revolver. He pulled the Rebbe out of the row and took him to his commander, accusing the Rebbe of "sabotage" and demanding that the Rebbe be killed.

The Rebbe did not flinch. It was a great and holy day, and he felt it was a great thing to be killed for observing Shabbos.

Suddenly, a miracle occurred. Another officer, seeing what was happening, called out to the Rebbe and shoved him back into the row of prisoners. The Rebbe continued marching, without a bundle.[5]

He did not, however, survive the incident unharmed. The Rebbe sustained a large bloody wound near his rib cage from the butt of the Nazi's gun, from which he suffered for many years.[6]

Parched with Thirst

As the sun rose in the sky, its fiery rays beat down on the prisoners. Those who tried to eat some bread could not swallow it because their mouths were so parched. As drops of sweat rolled off their foreheads into their mouths, their thirst increased. Every so often a prisoner fell to the ground – dead.

The prisoners passed cities and villages famous for their Jewish communities such as Sochatchov and Kotna. Now the Jewish populations had been completely eradicated. The sight of the *Judenrien* cities was heartbreaking.[7]

On the third day of the march, the Sunday observed as Tishah B'Av, the torture reached its zenith. From sunrise the SS

---

5 Reported by Menachem Mendel Weider.
6 Reported by Yehoshua Veitzenblum.
7 Reported by Meir Shraga Perdelsky in *Sefer Sosnowitz*.

guards intensified their beatings of the broken prisoners, using wooden clubs and steel bars like crazy men. More prisoners died that day than on any other day of the death march. Their corpses were left on the road without burial. The rows of prisoners gradually thinned.

They were mere skeletons, shadows of their former selves. They could hardly walk, particularly since most had removed their shoes because of the heat. They threw away whatever they could to lighten their loads. Their clothes stuck to their bodies; their faces were sunburned and covered with dust. With mouths full of the dust and dirt and tongues as dry as rubber, the prisoners were completely dehydrated.

One prisoner felt he could no longer continue. Opening his shirt and pointing to his heart, he screamed at an SS guard, "Give me a drink of water, or shoot me right now. I cannot go on like this."

Alas, neither request was granted. The guard struck the prisoner with a sudden and forceful blow on the head, and the dazed man returned to the rows of marchers.

Barefoot

The Rebbe also marched before his captors, as weak as the rest. The other prisoners had thrown their shoes away because of the terrible heat, but the Rebbe had removed his shoes earlier because it was Tishah B'Av and wearing leather shoes was prohibited as one of the five afflictions observed on that day. His internal *Shulchan Aruch* had reminded him to remove his shoes.

The Rebbe whispered to himself verses from *Eichah* and *Kinos*. Suddenly, one of the guards came up to him, singling him out from among the other barefoot prisoners, and ordered him out of the line. He told the Rebbe to march on the shoulder of the road, among the gravel and broken glass.[8]

After a few minutes, the Rebbe tried something daring. Hoping that he would not be detected, he bent down and rolled into a ditch by the side of the road. The long line of prisoners had nearly passed him when the SS guards spotted him and began shooting in his direction. One bullet hit the Rebbe's arm, which began to bleed.

The Rebbe made a lightning-quick calculation and decided the danger of trying to escape was far greater than the danger of returning to the march. However, if the Nazis saw that he was wounded, they would likely finish him off. Pulling some wet leaves off a nearby tree, he bandaged his wound and quickly rejoined the rows of prisoners. Once again the Rebbe's life had been saved.[9]

The River

When the prisoners were finally on the verge of collapse, one of the guards barked out an order to move off the main road. "Turn left, rest!" An electric current passed through the rows of prisoners at the word *rest*. Their eyes lit up when they beheld the river they were being directed to. They were ordered to sit down on the riverbank and wait.

---

8 Reported by Shimon Michel Shemaya, who heard it from the Rebbe.
9 See the *Sanz* newspaper, vol. 260 (*Erev Rosh HaShanah* 1996), p. 22. The Rebbe related this story when the cornerstone for the Sanz-Laniado Hospital was laid (July 29, 1980) and said that he decided at that time that when he survived the war he was going to try to establish a medical center for Jews.

But who could wait when he was dying of thirst? The prisoners raced to the river to quench their thirst without waiting for an order from the guards.

A barrage of bullets rang out. The murderous Nazi guards raised their machine guns and shot at the prisoners at the river's edge. The blood of the pitiful Jews streamed into the river.

The march commander explained to the survivors with a satanic smile that he was forced to kill the prisoners because of his "sense of responsibility" and "compassion" for those who weren't careful enough and were likely to drown in the river. His underlings viciously ordered the other inmates to get up, return to formation, and begin marching again.

The Rebbe and Mendel Weider, unharmed by the shooting, managed to slip off for a few moments to some trees at the edge of the field near the river. They sucked some drops of water off the tree leaves and branches to wet their tongues and lips, but made sure not to swallow even a drop of water. It was Tishah B'Av. Who could eat and drink on that day?

Water at Last

After quenching their thirst at the river, the cruel guards led the marchers back onto the road. Several prisoners fell to the ground to lick the wet mud, filling their mouths with dirty water in which frogs and worms had crawled. They paid dearly for this moment of "pleasure" – the guards pounded their heads with the butts of their rifles and forced them back into the rows of marchers.

As a result of the river incident, the guards attacked the prisoners with renewed anger and fury. Meting out beatings right and left indiscriminately, they screamed, "Run! Run!" The terrified prisoners did as they were told, without even a moment to breathe.

Night came. An open field was selected as a campsite. When the signal was given, the prisoners fell to the wet ground like broken tree limbs. Exhausted and dehydrated, they could not fall asleep. Those who still had a grain of desire to live dipped the edges of their shirts into the saturated ground on which they sat and sucked the moisture out, over and over again.

The night was dark. The moon's silver light was obscured by clouds. The beaten marchers were surrounded by armed SS guards who had fallen asleep at their posts.

A whisper quickly rustled through the prisoners surrounding the Rebbe. "*He* says to try.... Everyone should dig beneath himself. God's salvation comes in the blink of an eye."

A glimmer of hope was kindled among the downtrodden Jews.

During the three days of the march, the Rebbe had pleaded with the prisoners not to drink from the dirty puddles on the roadside. "Do not drink that dirty water. You are poisoning yourself with your own hands," the Rebbe cautioned, begging for restraint.[10] Now that the Rebbe had given a positive command about the water, the prisoners had faith in him. Everyone began to dig — some with spoons, some with pieces of wood, others with their fingers and fingernails.

At first there were only a few small holes. Then the holes became larger, three inches, six, ten. And then, the water began to

10 Reported by Menachem Mendel Weider.

flow in small spurts. As the water appeared, joy engulfed the camp.

The following is the description of the event in K. Charmatz's book *Kashmaren*: "We were afraid to speak loudly lest the Nazis hear us, but in everyone's eyes a flame had been lit. Water. Fresh water.... Prisoners hugged and kissed each other out of joy and happiness. Half-dead Jews were returned to life in a moment. Feverishly, they dug more and more, deeper and deeper. The spurts of water grew stronger and stronger.

"Devout Jews, their lips as black as coal, gave thanks to Hashem, blessing and praising God. But while their lips moved, their voices could not be heard. Silently, they recited the blessing *Shehakol Nihiyeh Bidvaro*.

"Springs of water shot up everywhere. The thousands of prisoners gulped down the water until their thirst was quenched and their exhausted limbs were refreshed....

"Suddenly, an SS guard awoke and looked at us with a moronic look on his face. He stared for a few long moments until he understood what was happening. Quickly, he called out to the other guards. They jumped up immediately and ran to the crowd of prisoners to see what was going on. But they were too late to do anything.

"It seemed that they were afraid of starting a commotion in the middle of the night in unknown territory, out of concern that we would attack them. In the morning, when the march commander and other officers were brought to the camp and saw the miracle of the water, they were far from pleased. The night guards shrugged their shoulders and hurriedly left the area in shame."[11]

---

11 This story is related by Lida and Perdelsky in *Sefer Sosnowitz*, pp. 208, 242.

After the war, when one of the Rebbe's followers, Avraham Elyakim Getzel Schiff, heard of this amazing story, he asked the Rebbe, "Is it true?"

The Rebbe answered, "If anyone doubted, *chas veshalom*, the Torah's stories about Avraham Avinu's ram or Miriam's well, he saw clearly on that day the Master of the Universe truly provides for His creations precisely what they need, exactly when they need it."

From the moment of the miracle of the water, the Rebbe renewed his efforts to encourage those close to him. "Despite all our suffering and the *hester panim*, we see that HaKadosh Baruch Hu still loves us," he would say.[12]

The Fourth Day

On the fourth day of the march, the prisoners neared the town of Lubitch. A bit stronger after drinking the water that they had happily discovered the night before, they made their way at a renewed pace. The guards, however, continued their cruel kicks, beatings, and curses. The despicable *Kapos* picked on the weaker prisoners and terrorized those who could not keep up with the pace. Many of the marchers simply wanted to die.

At nightfall they reached the valley between Lubitch and Zhichlin. The prisoners were told that they would camp there for the night and on the next day they would be loaded onto trains that would take them to Dachau. After four days of hunger and thirst, the guards distributed some bread and salty horse-meat sausage, along with some black water which they called "coffee."

12 Reported by Yaakov Kahn.

As soon as the exhausted prisoners had fallen asleep, the world around them suddenly began to shake. In place of the oppressive heat of the past few days, ominous clouds covered the sky. In a minute the heavens lit up with streaks of lightning, accompanied by loud thunder.

Within seconds, it began to storm violently. The cold wind carried away the prisoners' thin blankets and left them chilled to the bone. There was no place to take cover. The prisoners were forbidden to get up; anyone who even raised his head was immediately greeted by a barrage of bullets.

The prisoners huddled together and tried to warm up, covering themselves with whatever they could find — rags, torn coats, leaves. But to no avail. Rain poured down, filling the entire valley. The guards, armed with their clubs and revolvers, stood ready to strike or shoot anyone who tried to get out. Feverish from the intense heat of the day, the prisoners were now shivering from the sudden cold. Just the day before they had yearned for a drop of water, and now they were almost drowning.

Morning came and the commanders, rested and dry, wearing stylish raincoats, arrived to inspect the prisoners. They surveyed the living dead before them with wide smiles and barked out, "Step forward!"

The SS guards, assisted by the *Kapos*, hurried the prisoners into rows so that they could be searched before the train ride.

The prisoners could hardly move a limb or take a single step. But the whips and curses quickly made it obvious that they were not going to receive any consideration from their oppressors. Although an announcement was made that they were searching only for knives and spoons, the Nazis forced each prisoner to empty his bag and confiscated almost everything. Even the pair of damaged tefillin that the Rebbe and a handful of others had been donning secretly every day were taken.

Entering the Cattle Cars

When the search was over, the prisoners marched to the rail station in Zhichlin, where empty cattle cars awaited them. They were pushed into the cars with extraordinary brutality. Each car could fit at most only forty people, but ninety to a hundred prisoners were crammed into each one. Inside the cars, the prisoners were divided up, half in each side of the car. The middle of the car, the area opposite the door, was occupied by two armed SS guards and one *Kapo*, who stretched out comfortably in the space allotted to them.

After the prisoners were pushed into the cattle cars at a murderous pace, the train did not move for several long hours. No explanation was offered to the prisoners. It was later discovered that some of their members had tried to escape and the guards were searching for them.

During these long hours, the Rebbe stood in a corner, deep in prayer. Suddenly, shots rang out. The Rebbe was startled, the sound having brought him back to reality. Before long he saw puddles of blood around him and realized suddenly that his clothing was also splattered with blood. He realized that it was a miracle that he himself had not been hurt.[13]

---

13 Reported by Mendel Weider.

The Death Train

Finally the train was ready to leave. The doors were locked and the guards distributed food for the trip: half a loaf of bread per person, a spoonful of margarine, and salty sausage links. The train's horn blew, and the train began to move.

The SS guards and *Kapos* immediately began cursing, beating, and spitting at the prisoners. Throwing clubs and other weapons at them, they would immediately demand to have their weapons returned so that the cruel game could begin again.

The air was filled with a terrible stench from both living and dead bodies. Many of the prisoners died on the train, either from starvation or by being trampled in the overcrowded car. The dead bodies were piled in the corners so that the living could spread out or sit on the pile of corpses. There was simply nowhere else to sit. They stood the entire journey, awake, asleep, eating, and relieving themselves.

Some of the prisoners lost their sanity. All of them were terribly thirsty, especially after consuming the salty sausage, and the thirstier they were, the weaker they became. Some extracted gold teeth from their mouths and traded them with the *Kapos* for a drink of water.

Upon occasion, when the train stopped, the guards went out and returned with jugs of water, which they put in the middle of the cars. The prisoners raced to get some water, but most of it spilled on the floor because of the disorder. At other times, when the train stopped near springs of water, some of the prisoners were allowed to go out. At the end of their strength, they ran toward the water — but the Germans let their attack dogs loose, claiming that they had to prevent the prisoners from escaping. The dogs viciously attacked the prisoners and many did not survive.

Despite the inhuman conditions of the journey, the Rebbe remained as noble as ever. Exercising superhuman restraint, he stood the entire journey. In addition to extreme respect for the dead who had been piled up in the corner of the rail car — refusing to even move into the area where the corpses had been piled — the Rebbe was very respectful of the living. He never pushed or squeezed a fellow prisoner and was careful not to step on anyone else, even accidentally. Every one of his movements was measured, in the manner of royalty.[14]

Baruch Ganz, a follower of the Rebbe, recalled, "I stood next to the Rebbe in the railcar and heard him reciting *divrei Torah* at the time that he calculated was *shalosh seudos* on Shabbos. The rest of us had long since lost track of the days of the week, but the Rebbe had not."

Years later the Rebbe related that during the entire train ride, surrounded by people dying of dehydration, he thought to himself that when he would at last merit a sip of water he would recite the blessing *Shehakol Nihiyeh Bidvaro* with such concentration and intensity that the heavens would tremble.

In the end, he concluded sadly, with great humility, the blessing which he recited for that first drink did indeed have a *Yiddishe taam*, but with the passage of time his blessings had become habitual and lacked the same intensity. "Today, who among us knows how to really appreciate a drink of water?"[15]

---

14 Reported by Eliyahu Yaakov Steinmetz.
15 Reported by Moshe Sherer, who heard it from the Rebbe.

Dachau

Of the close to six thousand prisoners who left Warsaw, less than two thousand made it all the way to Dachau. The dazed prisoners who had survived the tortuous journey exited the cattle cars like wild creatures, half naked, filthy, and reeking, covered with wounds and bruises. The fresh air went to their heads like liquor to an alcoholic. Wobbling about on rubbery legs, their eyes racing from side to side, they hardly remembered their own names.

"*Arbeit macht frei* — work makes one free" read the sign over the entrance to the concentration camp, a tangible reminder of the Germans' hypocrisy. The prisoners were summoned to be counted and classified. Every prisoner was given a new number, the tattooed number from Auschwitz no longer valid.

The center of the Dachau camp was strewn with dead bodies and prisoners just barely alive, slowly wasting away. Suddenly, an announcement came over the loudspeaker: "Anyone who feels sick should come to register. The sick will be cared for separately from the other workers."

Many of the prisoners perked up at this announcement, not realizing it was just a ploy to exterminate those who could not work.

The Rebbe, recognizing the danger, darted in and out among the rows of prisoners waiting to be given a number and an assignment and whispered to everyone he could reach, "Don't sign up as sick! Don't sign up as sick!"

The Rebbe's warning soon spread throughout the crowd.

Yaakov Kahn recalled, "On the day of our arrival in Dachau, I heard the Rebbe saying, "Since HaKadosh Baruch Hu has kept us alive until now, even through the death and destruction of this journey, we will certainly merit to be saved and remain alive!"

During the first few days spent in Dachau, the prisoners managed to regain a little bit of strength, strength which they would need for the coming days. Then they were divided into groups and assigned to various forced labor camps near Dachau. The Rebbe was assigned to a labor group that was sent to work in the Muldorf Forest.

Chapter 7

The Muldorf Forest

Hell on Earth

For the next eight months the Klausenberger Rebbe was caught in the talons of the Nazis in Muldorf, a concentration and work camp approximately fifty miles from Munich. The concentration camp was divided into two sections: the main camp (*Shtamlager*), which served as the central point of assembly for all the forced laborers, and the forest camp (*Waldlager*), which was located in the middle of a large forest some fifteen kilometers from a village called Hempping.

In Dachau, the Rebbe had been assigned to the *Waldlager*, where the inmates were housed in temporary winter barracks, huts constructed of cardboard planks of wood, mostly underground. Only the roofs were above ground, and they were covered with soil to prevent rain and cold air from seeping in. Inside, the walls were lined with bunks, one on top of the next, with a small square space left empty in the middle of the hut. Each bunk contained a sack filled with a bit of straw which served as a mattress. A single small window above the entrance provided some light. These bunkers were scattered throughout the camp, which was surrounded by an electrified barbed wire fence.

The *Waldlager* laborers were put to work constructing a subterranean hangar and an airport and building missile batteries which the Germans intended to use for bombing large European cities like London. They spent twelve hours a day in backbreaking labor. In addition, getting to the construction site, a distance of five miles from the bunkers, was exhausting. Each day the Nazis forced the prisoners to march by foot, in wooden shoes, through the winding forest paths to the work site. Such a hike would have been difficult under any circumstances, but the return trip, after an entire day of hard labor, was nearly beyond the inmates' abilities. The SS guards, eager to return to their comfortably heated barracks, unhesitatingly used their whips to hurry the prisoners up. "Faster, Jews, faster!" they would scream.

Unimprisoned Spirit

Despite the torturous labor and work conditions, the oppression and deadly terror, the Rebbe's burning love for his Creator remained as strong as ever. The Nazis ruled over his physical being with great cruelty, but they had no control over his spirit and his soul. The Klausenberger was one of the freest men ensnared by the Nazi regime.

When the Rebbe's pain became almost intolerable, he exemplified a story told in the *Shevet Yehudah* (by Rav Shlomo Virga) about the saintly Jew among those expelled from Spain who suffered terribly from persecution and tragedies. Raising his hands to the heavens, he cried out one day, "Master of the

Universe, You are doing so much to make me abandon my faith. But I want You to know that I am a Jew and a Jew I shall remain, and nothing that You do to me will change that!"

In addition to maintaining his own human dignity and *kedushah*, the Rebbe was a powerful example from whom many other Jews drew their strength. Survivor Asher Brenner recalled, "Once while I was imprisoned in Muldorf a Jewish prisoner, a great Torah scholar who had been raised in Hungary, died in the infirmary. The Rebbe eulogized him publicly with great emotion. I will never forget the impression this eulogy made upon me. We were all indifferent to death. People dropped like flies all day, and those who were still alive were being trampled like worms. In the midst of this hell, the Rebbe uplifted the honor of a human being, a Jew who had been created in God's image."

An irreligious Jewish prisoner wrote: "The Klausenberger Rebbe was the only light in the darkness of the concentration camp. He stood head and shoulders above those around him. His tremendous influence radiated all around him, and he instilled in us great faith — that we should remain strong despite everything...and hope for a complete redemption. There were other rabbis and religious personalties among us, from all strains of the intelligentsia, but the Klausenberger Rebbe stood out among them all with his extraordinary behavior, pride in being Jewish, great dedication...prayers that broke our hearts...and his strict observance of every detail of Jewish law. Everyone loved him. He was greatly respected, even by the Germans."[1]

One of the Rebbe's block mates recalled that when they set out for work on Shabbos the Rebbe would tie his handkerchief

---

1 Quoted in *Sefer Sosnowitz*, vol. 2, p. 243.

around his neck so as not to carry it in a public domain. He would tell the Jews around him that while only a Rabbinic prohibition was involved in carrying because they were not walking in a biblical public domain, and they were forced to do *melachah d'oraisa* to save their lives throughout the day, in any event, they should be careful to avoid voluntarily desecrating Shabbos in every way possible.[2]

Another survivor, Tzvi Moskowitz, remembered how the Rebbe made every effort to study Torah even while walking to work. He would read Talmudic passages aloud from a torn page hidden in his clothes so that not only he but also those near him would be able to study Torah. "I tried to absorb what the Rebbe was reading and thus was able to forget, for a few moments, everything that was happening to us. Perhaps as a result of those few moments I was able to remain strong."

Nonstop Labor

The prisoners' main job was to carry heavy bags of cement on their backs to the huge cement mixers and empty them into the mixers, which operated nonstop, twenty-four hours a day. The prisoners were divided into two twelve-hour shifts. The day shift worked from six A.M. to six P.M., and the night shift worked from six P.M. to six A.M. They were shifted from day to night shifts every other week. All the prisoners preferred the day shift because the nights were extremely cold, especially during the winter, and they wore only their striped prisoner's uniforms, consisting of a shirt and pants. The Rebbe, however, preferred to

---

2 Reported in *Zichron Michael*, a book written in memory of Y. M. Youngerman (Zichron Yaakov, Israel, 1989).

work the night shift; so much so that even when he was assigned to the day shift he would try to change to the night shift.[3]

The labor was excruciatingly difficult and demoralizing. The prisoners had difficulty breathing because the cement dust filled their mouths and their nostrils, penetrating into their lungs. They frequently suffered from nausea and vomiting. But the *Kapos* and SS guards would not allow them even a moment's rest.

Every fifty prisoners was supervised by *Kapos*, work supervisors, and several SS guards. When a prisoner was caught resting, he was taken out to the forest and beaten to death.

A Tower of Bavel

A Muldorf survivor described the *Waldlager* as a "Tower of Bavel." "Many different languages were spoken there, and curses were uttered in every language imaginable, for this was a collection of laborers from many countries.... We could all cry the same tears, except that crying was impossible because our tears had completely dried up. Our hearts ached.... Hunger was a constant companion. Instead of food, we consumed cement dust....

"From time to time the Nazis conducted selections, removing the prisoners who were too weak to work and sending them to their deaths in the crematoria in Dachau."[4]

Human life was cheap in the *Waldlager*, like it was in the Tower of Bavel. Our Sages say (*Pirkei D'Rabbi Eliezer* 24) that when the Tower was being built, "If a person fell and died, they

---

3 Reported by David Greenzweig.
4 Charmatz, p. 212.

would not pay any attention to him. But if a brick fell they would sit and cry, 'When will a replacement brick be sent up'?" So it was in the *Waldlager*. A bag of spilled cement made a much greater impression than did the death of ten prisoners.

The Rebbe's Suffering

The Klausenberger Rebbe was assigned the job of carrying cement bags from the rail transports to the main construction site, a hangar. Each bag weighed 110 pounds, and the Rebbe had to carry them on his back and shoulders, hour after hour, without even a moment's rest.

The Rebbe was physically very weak. From time to time he would fall to the ground because of his hunger and weakness. But not a single one of his supervisors eased up on the quota. Once the Rebbe was so weak that he could not carry his heavy bag and lost his grip on it as he was lowering it to the ground. The bag fell and tore, causing some cement to spill out. The German work supervisors immediately rushed over and began to beat him viciously.[5]

On another occasion, during the daily roll call, the Rebbe was attacked by a *Kapo*. Although the Rebbe's followers usually tried to hide him in the middle rows so that he would not be spotted by the guards, Aharon Roth recalled, "One morning the Rebbe was called to stand in the front row. It was terribly cold and snowy that day. A young *Kapo*, a Jew by the name of Moishele, scrutinized the row and found the Rebbe's posture unacceptable. He slapped the Rebbe across the face and cursed him bitterly in Russian. Clearly he knew exactly who the Rebbe

---

5 Witnessed by Eliyahu Yaakov Steinmetz and Yaakov Kahn.

was, but his reasons for attacking the Rebbe remain a mystery."[6]

In Honor of Shabbos

When Shabbos came the Rebbe refused to carry any cement bags. It wasn't long before the Nazis saw that he wasn't working. Brandishing their pistols, they tried to force the Rebbe to desecrate Shabbos, but the Rebbe refused. The guards vented their anger by attacking the Rebbe with their fists and the butts of their guns. Still, they could not get him to budge.

Yaakov Eliezer Dirnfeld, another Muldorf prisoner, recalled, "I saw several times with my own eyes how the Rebbe refused to do *melachah* on Shabbos and how the Germans beat him viciously."

The Jews close to the Rebbe, including his barracks leader, were filled with compassion when they saw how weak he was and tried to ease his burden. One of them succeeded in bribing the German work supervisors into excusing the Rebbe from carrying the heavy cement bags. Instead, he was assigned the job of collecting spilled cement and putting it into an open container. German efficiency demanded that there not be even the slightest waste of any building materials. After the cement was gathered up, the Rebbe and another prisoner carried the container to the mixers.

Because the Rebbe did not have to carry the container by himself, he felt that his burden had been eased to a degree, not only physically, but also, more importantly, because he did not have to desecrate Shabbos. Together with one of his young followers, David Greenzweig, who had also been assigned to fill

6 Rabbi Isser Frankel, *Shearim* (24 Av, 1979).

and carry the container, he would employ various schemes to make it look as though he was working as usual even on Shabbos.[7]

One Shabbos, the Rebbe was caught. A particularly tyrannical *Kapo* named Zigi noticed that the Rebbe was avoiding Shabbos desecration and took it upon himself to punish the Rebbe. He ordered the Rebbe, under the threat of death, to return to the construction site in the forest and carry sacks full of cement by himself, without any assistance.

When the Rebbe returned to the barracks that night, near collapse, his clothes were torn and he breathed only with difficulty. His fellow prisoners barely recognized him. One of the prisoners, Moshe Eliezer Einhorn, quickly came to the Rebbe's assistance. Bathing the Rebbe and stealing some clean clothes from the warehouse for him, Moshe restored the Rebbe's spirit somewhat. When the Rebbe told him what had happened, Moshe went to report it to Mr. Heisler, a member of the camp secretariat. Heisler immediately punished Zigi for his cruelty toward the Rebbe.[8]

Easier Work

Some time after this incident, one of the Rebbe's fellow prisoners went to the camp management to ask for an easier work assignment for the Rebbe "By a miracle," the prisoner related, "they agreed to assign the Rebbe to maintenance work in the camp. The Rebbe went from barracks to barracks sweeping the floor and straightening out the wooden bunks, all the while

---

7 Reported by David Greenzweig.
8 Reported by Moshe Eliezer Einhorn.

praying to his heart's content. He knew of my intercession on his behalf and made sure to express his appreciation with warm and heartfelt thanks."[9]

Another prisoner who worked with the Rebbe after the winter barracks were built in the *Waldlager* related that they had long conversations about the past, the present, and the future which gave him encouragement.

Once, the head German supervisor discovered the Rebbe standing and praying *Shemoneh Esrei* and began to yell at him. When the Rebbe did not respond, the supervisor grew angrier and angrier. The Rebbe's coworker hurried over and explained that the Rebbe was a holy man. "He is our chief rabbi, and right now he's in the middle of praying."

A miracle occurred. The supervisor looked at the Rebbe and let slip, "Pray, Rabbi, pray.... But just for our victory."[10]

Illness and the Sock Shop

After only a short time, when the winter barracks were completed, the Rebbe was forced to return to hauling cement. Meir Shraga Perdelsky related, "Originally, the prisoners with torn shoes or inadequate clothing were exempt from work. But when the shoe and clothing situation in the *Waldlager* worsened, even the prisoners without shoes or clothes were sent to work at the construction site. The number of prisoners who died each day rose significantly, and there were not enough workers. The Klausenberger Rebbe fell ill and lay in his bunk for a long time."[11]

9 Charmatz, p. 225.
10 *Sefer Sosnowitz*, vol. 2, p. 243.
11 See note above.

As soon as he felt a little better, the Rebbe was forced to return to work. Moshe Eliezer Einhorn came to his rescue again and arranged to have him assigned to work in the sock shop. Because of his own disability, Moshe Eliezer served as a night watchman in the camp. He took advantage of every opportunity to ease the Rebbe's burden, sometimes obtaining a medical exemption for the Rebbe on Shabbos and sometimes getting the Rebbe an extra portion of bread or vegetables from the kitchen.[12]

The work in the sock shop was relatively easy for the Rebbe. Some of his fellow workers were careful, like himself, not to desecrate Shabbos, and on Shabbos they would hold needles and thread in their hands and pretend to sew. The Rebbe, for the most part, wouldn't even hold a needle on Shabbos because it was *muktzeh*.

One of his fellow workers, Alexander Dirnfeld,[13] recalled, "One Shabbos, some supervisors and important military officers came to inspect the shop. The Rebbe, realizing that it was a matter of life and death, searched feverishly for a needle to hold. I kept an extra needle hidden for emergencies. I pulled it out quickly and gave it to the Rebbe. As soon as the inspection was over and the inspectors left, the Rebbe dropped the needle onto the workshop table again."

Yet Another Beating

The camp rules required all inmates to have their heads and faces shaved by a specially designated barber. The Rebbe told

---

12 Reported by Moshe Eliezer Einhorn.
13 A brother of Yaakov Eliezer Dirnfeld, mentioned above.

the barber that while he would comply with the order, he wanted to be shaved only with a scissors or a shaving machine, not with a razor. When the barber insisted on shaving the Rebbe only with a razor, the Rebbe refused to allow his head and face to be shaved at all.

The barber promptly informed the authorities. The barracks leader began screaming at the Rebbe and beating him. The Rebbe, however, remained firm. When a German officer saw what was going on, he ran over, steaming with anger, and ordered the barber to remove the Rebbe's beard with the flesh because he would not stand for a prisoner's insanity.

The Rebbe broke down in tears and begged the officer not to shave his beard and instead to beat him. "I am willing to receive fifty lashes rather than have my beard shaved off!" he cried bitterly.

The Nazi ignored the Rebbe's pleading and immediately called two guards over, instructing them to strip the Rebbe's clothes off and beat him until he was willing to accept authority and be shaved.

The Rebbe submitted himself to the beating, his spirit was unbroken even as the blood spewed forth from his body. All the while, he whispered, "*U'vechol nafshecha* — even if He takes your life."

Suddenly a commanding officer appeared. For some unknown reason, he reacted to the scene with shock and ordered the guards to stop momentarily. "Why are you beating this prisoner?"

The Rebbe's oppressors explained the situation. To their great astonishment, the commanding officer's face twisted and he blurted out, "Leave him alone. Just use the scissors."[14]

---

14 Reported by Moshe Eliezer Einhorn, who personally witnessed the incident.

Surviving on Bread and Water

It is difficult to grasp the Rebbe's enormous spiritual strength during those terrible times. Eyewitnesses relate that the Rebbe was the only Jewish prisoner who never ate or drank any nonkosher food or any food cooked in the camp kitchen. He never even drank the "black coffee" that was distributed, let alone foods that had some possibility of being *treif* or of being cooked by non-Jews. For the entire nine months in Muldorf, the Rebbe lived on meager portions of bread and water. Sometimes, a fellow prisoner took the Rebbe's portion of cooked food from the camp kitchen and traded it for an extra piece of dry bread to supplement the Rebbe's "meal."

Even when it came to bread, the Rebbe observed various stringencies. A fellow prisoner in the *Waldlager* recalled that "The Rebbe was as careful with 'light' halachos as he was with 'strict' ones. On Shabbos he would not take anything with him so as not to transgress the prohibition against carrying on Shabbos. When I would give him bread, he would ask me from where I had obtained it. Only after I said that I had hidden it away for him on Friday did he accept it. Although this wasn't always true, I figured that in our situation saving the Rebbe's life nullified the normal prohibitions of Shabbos, and I was even willing to be punished in the World to Come for the sake of the Rebbe's health."[15]

In Other Prisoners' Eyes

One irreligious survivor recalled, "The Klausenberger

---

15 Meir Shraga Perdelsky in a letter to the author.

Rebbe was an extraordinary personality in Muldorf. Under no circumstances would he taste the soup or the piece of sausage given out once a week. He was very weak and his body shrank from day to day.

"Many in the camp grumbled to the Rebbe about his conduct and deprecated his behavior. Some argued that in such a situation every person was obligated to save his own life and not try to keep laws of *kashrus*. Others even suspected that the Rebbe was putting on an act to curry sympathy. There were those who belittled the Rebbe and tried angrily to 'educate' him by hitting him.

"But I understood that the Rebbe's intentions were genuine. He preferred death from starvation over defiling himself with nonkosher food. When others traded his food for him from time to time, he would get a dry piece of bread in return for his portion of soup and his sausage. He willingly allowed himself to be taken advantage in this way, for the value of the soup was far greater than the value of the bit of dry bread which he got in return. Often when no one was willing to trade, the Rebbe gave his soup away for free. Never would he eat it."[16]

As time passed, the prisoners gained respect and awe for the Rebbe's insistence on eating kosher food only, and some had pity on him and tried to help. Eliezer Dirnfeld recalled the following: "I was a teenager at the time and therefore not required to do the hard labor at the construction site. Instead, I was assigned to work in the camp kitchen peeling potatoes. Ignoring the great danger, from time to time I would pocket a carrot, a small radish, or a potato for the Rebbe. If I had been caught, I

16 Charmatz, p. 224.

would almost certainly have been killed. But I was not the only Jew who did this for the Rebbe. Anyone who was able to get some raw vegetables for him did so."

Another survivor related, "Because I had some connections in the kitchen, I often tried to get a piece of bread or some raw potatoes for the Rebbe…. Sometimes I would ask the cook for the donation of a potato, a carrot, or the head of a beet for the holy man from Klausenberg. I felt that I was sustaining his life."[17]

Washing His Hands

Alexander Dirnfeld related, "Of course, the Rebbe completely refrained from eating nonkosher food while he was imprisoned and survived on stale bread. I myself traded his soup for bread among other prisoners. But what was really incredible was that even when the Rebbe finally got a small piece of bread with which to still his hunger, he would not eat it until after he had washed his hands. Sometimes he would wait even a day or two before he got some water."

David Greenzweig added, "Many times I saw the Rebbe standing next to the concrete mixer for hours at a time with an empty can in his hand, collecting the drops of water that dripped from the tank." The Rebbe had no other way to get water, neither in the camp nor at the work site. The water that the Germans distributed to each prisoner was not enough, and the puddles of rainwater that collected on the ground in the camp courtyard and in the forest always froze. Those around the Rebbe were completely astounded when they learned that the

17 Ibid.

water that the Rebbe was collecting was not for drinking but, rather, to wash his hands before eating or davening.

On one occasion, a religious prisoner somehow obtained several bottles of water. The Rebbe went and asked him for a little bit of it. The man was uncertain what to do. After thinking the situation over, he said to the Rebbe, "Water is very scarce. If you need the water to wash your hands so that you can eat, I will gladly give it to you, but if you need it for *hiddurim* and stringencies, then even according to the opinion of Ben Petura I am not required to give it to you."[18]

The Rebbe answered, "I want to eat...." The man immediately gave him the water. "But I have not yet davened," the Rebbe continued, "and it is forbidden to eat before praying. In order for me to be permitted to eat I must first daven. I will wash my hands prior to praying so that I may eat afterwards."

The Rebbe used the water to wash his hands. Of course, after he finished he had no water left with which to wash his hands before eating, and therefore he did not eat anything that day. But for the Rebbe, washing his hands for davening took precedence over eating. Spiritual nourishment was more important to his survival than physical nourishment.[19]

Two Loaves for Shabbos

Kind Jews looked out for the Rebbe and made sure that he had something to eat. But the Rebbe's concern was, first and

---

18 The Gemara in *Bava Metzia* (62a) records the opinion of Ben Petura that if two people are walking in the desert with only enough water to sustain one of them, they must share the water. The halachah, however, follows Rabbi Akiva, who rules that only the one who has the water should drink.
19 Reported by Alexander Dirnfeld.

foremost, for his spiritual needs, as the verse says, "Not on bread alone can man live." As Shabbos approached each week, the Rebbe did his utmost to obtain two challos in honor of the holy day. Even though he never had enough bread to satisfy his hunger, he had to have two challos over which to recite Kiddush and to eat the Shabbos meal.

The Germans distributed daily portions of bread to the prisoners in whole loaves, one loaf for six prisoners. Every evening when they returned from the hard labor, the prisoners stood in line for their loaves of bread, which they then divided up among themselves. The Rebbe searched for five volunteers each week who would agree to forgo Thursday's loaf and keep it whole until Friday night, when they would get a second loaf. Then they would use both loaves as challah for Shabbos and eat them both.

It should be noted, however, that sometimes the Rebbe would notice that one of his five volunteers looked ravenous or very weak. The Rebbe would slice the bread immediately and urge the prisoner to eat it so that he would get stronger, even though it meant that the Rebbe would not have his *lechem mishneh*.[20]

Concerns of His Own

The many recollections of Muldorf survivors combine to provide a clear and detailed picture of the Rebbe during that very difficult time. Despite the satanic cruelty to which he was constantly subjected, the Rebbe was concerned only with serving Hashem and fulfilling the Torah and mitzvos. His obligations to the Almighty were the same whether he was sitting com-

---

20 Reported by Moshe Tuvia Greenzweig.

fortably and peacefully as the leader of Klausenberg Jewry or whether he was being trampled beneath the feet of the Nazi oppressors.

Many years later, the Rebbe related to his followers, "There were three mitzvos that were the most difficult for Jewish prisoners to fulfill." He went on to explain each one in detail:

The night-time recitation of Shema during the summer, when nightfall was very late, was very difficult for the prisoners. They were forced to retire to their bunks at an early hour and were prohibited from uttering a sound. Since they were exhausted and drained from the day's work, they fell asleep quickly. Thus, it was difficult for them to observe the mitzvah of reciting the Shema at its proper time.

The mitzvah of *kiddush levanah* was also difficult. In order to recite the blessing, one had to leave the barracks and look at the moon, but it was absolutely forbidden to go out at night and anyone who did so would with pay with his life.

Finally, the mitzvah of counting the Omer was beyond the abilities of most prisoners. For the most part, the prisoners were confused and disoriented, and they had entirely lost the concept of time. If not for the fact that the Rebbe repeated to himself all day long that "today is such-and-such day of the Omer," he would not have been able to count the Omer either.[21]

Lighting Chanukah Candles

The Rebbe once described how he was able to light Chanukah candles while imprisoned in Muldorf and the miracles he experienced as a result: "It just so happened that shortly

---

21 Reported by Rabbi Asher Reich, who heard it from the Rebbe.

before Chanukah, I was assigned to work in the camp wood warehouse. With the assistance of several other Jewish prisoners, I secretly made a wooden menorah. One member of the group obtained oil and wicks from the Germans. [It is rumored that the oil was margarine stored up for the daily rations, and the wicks were threads separated from the prisoners' clothing.]

"When the first night of Chanukah arrived, I merited to light the first light. We were extremely happy.

"On one of the following nights, however, the candles started a fire and the barracks went up in flames. [The rumor has it that this occurred on Friday night; thus the prisoners could do nothing to stop it.] The Nazis immediately investigated to discover the cause of the fire. They would surely kill the prisoner who dared to commit such an act. Through the kindness of Hashem, however, I was saved from their hands."

The Rebbe paused for a moment and then continued with great emotion, "Even if I were to thank Hashem every day of my life, morning and night, I will never be able to thank Him for enabling me to fulfill the mitzvah of lighting the Chanukah candles as required. Not only that, but I also survived despite the great danger that surrounded me at that time."[22]

Perfect Faith

The Rebbe was often heard saying that he did not doubt Hashem's mercy in the slightest. He did not have even the slightest complaint or question as to why it was decreed that he should suffer so much and lose all his loved ones. "Hashem is perfect and all His ways are just," he would say. Hashem's kind-

---

22 Related at *seudah shelishis* on *Shabbos Parashas Vayeitzei*, 1983.

nesses are hidden and one must accept what happens with love.

In addition, one must always remember that the *Shechinah* is in exile along with the Jewish people; the fate of one is inextricably intertwined with the fate of the other, as the Sages teach (*Chagigah* 5a): The Jewish people have been decreed to suffer Divine concealment. Thus, if a person expects not to experience Divine concealment, this is a sign that he is not of Jewish origin.

The Rebbe typically did not say very much, spending most of his time in prayer or reciting psalms. His fiery black eyes were always awash with tears. Even when he went to work at the construction site he would frequently hide in the thick trees of the forest and pour out his heart in prayer.

Yet when the Rebbe saw someone who had lost all hope and needed encouragement, he stopped his activities to offer him private words of *chizzuk* and *emunah*. He would quote the words of the Sages about suffering and relate teachings from sacred books which would soothe the prisoner's soul.[23]

The Rebbe would also discuss complex *divrei Torah* from memory with a learned Jew named Rabbi Moshe Dov Baron of Lithuania, who by divine providence had made it to Muldorf alive after the majority of Lithuanian Jewry had been exterminated three to four years earlier.[24]

Working Nights

As mentioned above, when he was forced to work at the construction site, the Rebbe always tried to be assigned to the night shift. Even when he was assigned to the day shift, he

---

23 Reported by Moshe Weiss.
24 Reported by Aharon Baron, Reb Moshe Dov's son.

switched with other prisoners so that he could work at night. Even though the night shift was much more strenuous, the Rebbe preferred to spend the day hours in the camp so that he could don his tefillin at the right time. He would spend hours alone in his barracks, praying without disturbance.

The day workers left for work before dawn and returned to the camp after nightfall, when it was too late to don tefillin. A few prisoners managed to put on tefillin during the five-mile march to the work site. While the guards were still rubbing sleep from their eyes, they quickly took turns donning the one pair of tefillin in the possession of Reb Moshe Dov Baron.[25]

There were several pairs of tefillin secretly stowed away in the *Waldlager* at the prisoners' great personal risk. Over time, however, the Nazis confiscated and destroyed all of them except for the Rebbe's. His tefillin were the only ones to survive until liberation.

At first, the Rebbe would lend his tefillin to anyone who asked. During the long summer days many prisoners, upon their return from the construction site, were able to don the tefillin before nightfall and recite the first verse of Shema. When the days grew shorter and the workers returned to the camp after dark, they would go to the Rebbe's barracks and ask him for permission to put the tefillin on without a blessing.

In the following months, however, after several altercations with the guards, the Rebbe became concerned that his tefillin would be confiscated and stopped lending them out. Instead, he allowed prisoners to put them on only in his presence.[26]

25 Reported by Aharon Baron.
26 Reported by Moshe Weiss.

Mitzvos with Mesiras Nefesh

Many years later, when the Rebbe was telling his followers about events of the war years, he declared, "In Heaven, they wanted us Jews to perform mitzvos with *mesiras nefesh*."[27]

The Rebbe's followers in Muldorf saw clearly how the Rebbe lived the words of the Sages: "In the path that a person wishes to walk he is led" (*Makos* 10b). He was blessed with a unique measure of divine providence, which enabled him to fulfill all the mitzvos in every detail, even in the Nazi hell. Amazingly, he was able to fulfill even *minhagim* like eating an apple on the night of Rosh HaShanah and eating fruit on Tu B'Shevat. Of course, he ate matzah on the seder night even though baking it was extremely risky and posed great danger.

As Alexander Dirnfeld related, "We saw them in every instance that Hashem 'guards the feet of His righteous ones.' The Rebbe was guided from above so that he would be able to fulfill every mitzvah that it was possible to fulfill in the Muldorf camp.

The Rebbe once explained the Talmudic passage, "He who comes to purify is assisted" (*Yoma* 38b), as meaning that when a person is helped by heaven in observing his faith it is a clear sign that the person possessed pure intentions in the first place. This was an apt description of the Rebbe himself.

---

27 Reported by Rabbi Avraham Elazar Heskel, who heard it personally from the Rebbe.

Chapter 8

The High Holidays in the Shadow of Death

Rosh HaShanah

As the Yamim Noraim approached, the Rebbe spoke secretly to his fellow prisoners about gathering to daven together on Rosh HaShanah and Yom Kippur — despite the great danger.

Survivors have related that "it was clear from just looking at the Rebbe that the Day of Judgment was approaching. His face was grave and full of awe at the holiness of the day. His eyes seemed to gaze off into the distance, and his lips murmured constantly. He looked like a person preparing himself for an imminent and very important court case."[1]

On the day before Rosh HaShanah, the news spread throughout the camp that the Rebbe would be davening that evening in the round barracks, a large barracks which was one of the first built in Muldorf. At the time it was empty, no longer used as living quarters.

---

1 Charmatz, p. 225.

At nightfall, the exhausted prisoners returned from the construction site and hurried to the round barracks. Hundreds of them crowded in, prisoners from just about every barracks. The Rebbe began his stirring prayers, prayers that split the heavens, although he did not raise his voice lest the guards hear. His listeners could barely make out the words he uttered, for they were choked in his throat. The only thing that could be heard in the room were his sobs and broken sighs, accompanied by the silent tears of the assembled Jews.[2]

"After davening," related David Greenzweig, "we wished each other 'kesivah v'chasimah tovah' and 'shanah tovah' and returned to our barracks. My brother, Moshe Tuvia, who slept in the same barracks as the Rebbe, followed the Rebbe see if he would be making Kiddush. Sure enough, the Rebbe made Kiddush over bread and recited the blessing 'Asher Bachar Banu — Who Has Chosen Us from All Nations' with great emotion. He continued with Shehechiyanu, again with great intensity. 'Who has kept us alive, sustained us, and brought us to this season...' as though he was standing at his table with his chassidim in Klausenberg and not imprisoned by the satanic Nazi regime."

An Apple for Shehechiyanu

On the second night of Rosh HaShanah, the same scene repeated itself. The Rebbe led the tefillos in the barracks with the same intensity and afterwards recited Kiddush. To the surprise of the prisoners who stayed behind to hear Kiddush, the Rebbe recited Shehechiyanu on the second night as well, with enormous feeling and devotion.

2 Reported by David Greenzweig.

Why did the Rebbe recite *Shehechiyanu* a second time? The Rebbe had made the blessing over a fresh apple that would have been the pride of a Jewish table on an ordinary Rosh HaShanah.

Aryeh Lida recalled, "In Muldorf I worked as a shoemaker, which had been my trade for years. I was given various privileges, including better food. On *erev Rosh HaShanah* the Rebbe asked if I could get him an apple so that he could recite a *Shehechiyanu* over it. I did as he asked and brought him an apple. Afterwards I found out that the Rebbe did not eat the entire apple himself. Instead, he gave it to the sick prisoners in the infirmary."[3]

Raise Your Voice Like a Shofar

On the second day of Rosh HaShanah, many Jews gathered to spend some time with the Rebbe. One prisoner stood guard to warn them if a Nazi approached. The prisoners had no siddurim or *machzorim*, but the Rebbe recited the prayers by heart and others repeated them after him.

They had no shofar to blow, but the Rebbe made up for the lack as he expounded on the day's significance to the many prisoners gathered around him. The verse states, "Blessed is the nation that knows the sound of the shofar; they walk in the light of Your countenance, God." Although they did not have the shofar, the prisoners were able to fulfill the second half of the verse, walking in the light of the Almighty's countenance even in the valley of death.

The Rebbe spoke with a fiery spirit. He called to each prisoner to strengthen his faith, since they were all children of God.

---

3 *Sefer Sosnowitz*, vol. 2, p. 208.

Surely, in the same way that a father has mercy on his children, so God would have mercy on them. The redemption would soon come in the blink of an eye. "We must have faith in Hashem that, without any doubt, we will outlive all our enemies," he said.[4]

Kol Nidrei Night

A survivor movingly described the Klausenberger Rebbe's prayers on the night of *Kol Nidrei* in Muldorf: "All kinds of Jews from all sections of the camp came to *Kol Nidrei*. Although it was kept secret, anyone who found out about the prayers came to join. I'm sure that everyone at that *Kol Nidrei* in the *Waldlager* will never forget it as long as he lives."[5]

The Rebbe began with a low, sorrowful groan that emanated from the depths of his soul. "K-o-o-o–l Nidrei" reverberated throughout the barracks. The prisoners joined in with their own cries, which in a moment became a haunting wailing. Over the thunderous cries rose the Rebbe's voice as he continued, "*Ve'eisarei, u'shevuei, vecharamei....*" Tears streamed down everyone's face; the prisoners could not contain themselves anymore.

Every prisoner thought of previous *Kol Nidrei* nights — at home in their hometowns, among family, in shul. No one knew what had become of his family or his shul. Nor did he have any way of knowing what was in store for him. Would he survive this hell? They sobbed bitterly, rivers of tears streaming down their faces, unable to stop.

Only the Rebbe's spirit was unbroken. With each repetition

4 Reported by Aharon Baron.
5 Charmatz, p. 225.

of *Kol Nidrei*, his voice grew stronger and stronger. When he recited the phrase, "From this Yom Kippur until the next Yom Kippur, which comes upon us for good," his voice rang out with confidence, as though he was announcing glad tidings. The prisoners felt that he was guaranteeing that they would live to the next Yom Kippur, which would come upon them for good. To them it seemed that the Rebbe was capable of changing Hashem's decree. In a clear, comforting, and pleasant voice he completed the *Kol Nidrei*, drawing out the final words: "*Shevikin, shevisin, beteilin u'mevutalin, la sheririn v'la kayamin.*"

The prisoners, absorbed in their thoughts, did not notice the barracks leader approaching. He asked, "What's going on here?"

When they explained, the barracks leader understood, for he was also a prisoner. But he asked that the prisoners disperse because the SS guards were likely to notice the large assembly of prisoners and think that it was a demonstration against the camp commanders.

With aching hearts, the crowd dispersed. That night, as the prisoners lay on their bunks, the Rebbe's prayers echoed in their ears: "The next Yom Kippur, which comes upon us for good."

Hungry for the Word of God

Not all the prisoners went to their bunks to sleep for the night. Later, in the dark of night, some returned and gathered around the Rebbe, hungering to hear the word of God. The Rebbe spoke to them with great emotion about the meaning of Yom Kippur.

Yaakov Eliezer Dirnfeld recalled that night: "The passage of time has caused me to forget the specific words the Rebbe uttered, but the strong impact of that speech remains alive within me. In Muldorf, from time to time, people lost their ability to think clearly, if not their sanity. Their thoughts were consumed by their pain and suffering — how can I reduce the pain or get some more food?

"And then, all of a sudden, we heard the Rebbe speak of spiritual matters, about a Jew and his God, 'For on this day He shall atone for you..... Before Hashem you shall be purified....' The Rebbe spoke of subjects that we were not able to focus on our own."

A Miserable Sukkos

The seven days of Sukkos, "*zeman simchaseinu*," were terribly difficult for the Rebbe. He had no sukkah, no *esrog*, no *lulav*, and no *ushpizin*. Forty years later during a lecture in Jerusalem,[6] the Rebbe recalled bitterly, "I was in the camps on the Yamim Noraim and Sukkos. We were forced to do hard labor. Our evil oppressors removed the yarmulkes from our heads and took away the few siddurim and *machzorim* that we had so that we would not be able to daven. Could we possibly serve God there? Did we have a sukkah? Was it even in the realm of possibility for us to have one there?"

But no one could take away from the Rebbe the holiday of Shemini Atzeres, the special day when Hashem communes exclusively with the Jewish people. This day is the crowning jewel of all holidays, the climax of the Yamim Noraim and Sukkos, the

6 *Parashas Ki Savo*, 1984.

he Rebbe with his brothers before the war.

The Rebbe distributing Chanukah *gelt*.

The Rebbe on *erev Pesach*.

The Rebbe making Havdalah.

The Rebbe on Sukkos in Union City.

The Rebbe on Purim.

The Rebbe with a dreidel on Chanukah.

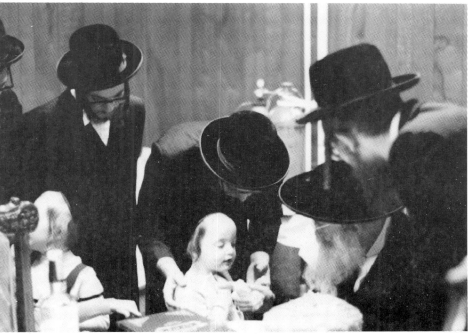

The Rebbe at an *upsherin.*

The Rebbe dancing a *mitzvah tantz*.

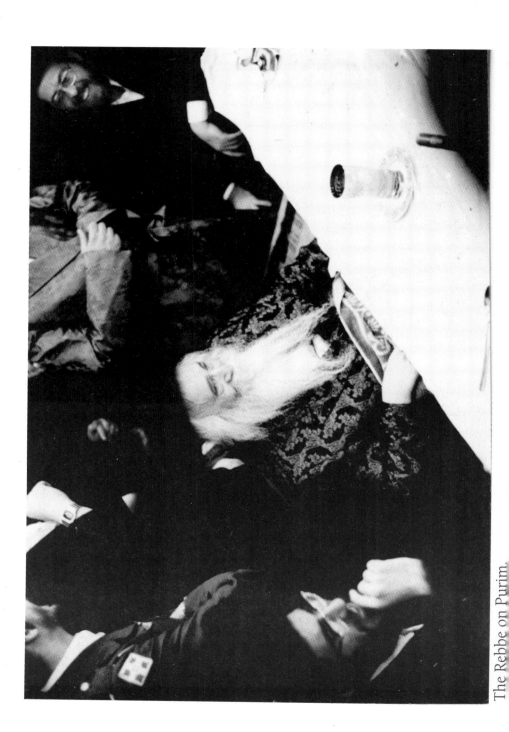

The Rebbe on Purim.

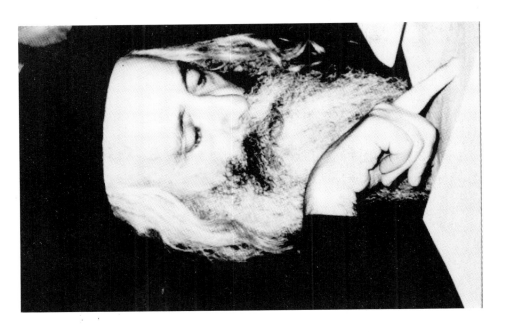
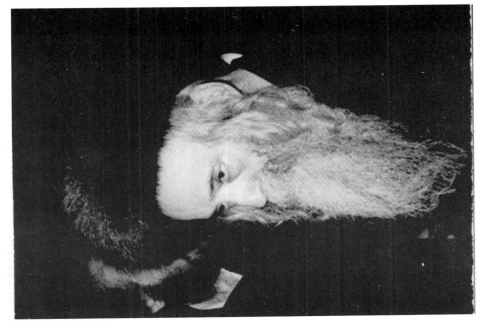

The Rebbe on Chanukah in Union City.

day when Hashem says to the Jewish people, "Come and let us celebrate, you and Me together."

Typically, on Shemini Atzeres the Rebbe's thoughts were on lofty spiritual matters. As the Maggid of Koznitz said, Shemini Atzeres is on a higher level than Shavuos, since our Sages taught, "Greater is the day of rain [Shemini Atzeres, on which we recite the prayer for rain] than the day the Torah was given."

Although the Rebbe was a prisoner of the Nazis, he would not give up his Shemini Atzeres celebration. The camp doctor, Dr. Greenbaum, a Jew by birth, had agreed to give the Rebbe an exemption from work because he required rest. Thus the Rebbe was able to spend the entire Sukkos in the infirmary. He planned to stay in the infirmary for Shemini Atzeres, as well.

A Change of Plans

On Hoshana Rabbah, Moshe Eliezer Einhorn, who had obtained the Rebbe's medical exemption for him, was informed privately that on the following day the *Oberfuehrer*, the senior commander, was coming to conduct a special inspection and selection. Together with him would be a certain Dr. Plukan, a very evil woman who was known for her practice of immediately separating out the weak and sick and sending them to the crematoria in Dachau. It was imperative for anyone who wanted to remain alive to show up for work and prove that he was strong and capable of working. Woe to anyone who was missing at roll call! Moshe Eliezer immediately became very concerned for the welfare of the Klausenberger Rebbe.

Moshe Eliezer hurried to Dr. Greenbaum and asked him to add the Rebbe to the list of those assigned to work for the next day. The doctor was surprised by the sudden request, since he was prepared to do the opposite, but Moshe Eliezer insisted. Although he could not explain why, the Rebbe could not be excused from work the following day.[7]

"I Will Not Work on Shemini Atzeres!"

When the Rebbe found out that evening that he was not excused from work on the following day, Shemini Atzeres, he was understandably extremely upset. Since he did not know why he had been reassigned to a work detail, he said firmly to himself, "No matter what happens to me, I will not go to work on Shemini Atzeres!" He remained in the barracks and davened to Hashem in the spirit of the day. But when the prisoners were inspected and counted, it became clear that a prisoner was missing.

Immediately guards were sent to look for the missing prisoner. They found the Rebbe standing in his barracks, deep in prayer, and dragged him to the prisoner lineup. There they proceeded to handcuff him and two guards beat him mercilessly in front of all the rest of the prisoners. When they finished, the Rebbe was so badly hurt that he was barely breathing. He was taken to the infirmary for immediate medical attention.

The poor Jews who witnessed this scene went to work, certain that the Rebbe had not survived the beating. When they came back at night, they were astonished to find the Rebbe not only alive, but back in his own barracks. He was limping around a small stool, holding a few pages from a small torn *Mishnayos* in his hand.

---

7 Reported by Moshe Eliezer Einhorn.

This was the Rebbe's *hakafos* in honor of Simchas Torah.[8]

Emerging Victorious

The prisoners were extremely moved by the sight of the Rebbe conducting *hakafos* after the brutal beating he had endured that morning. Even assimilated Jews in the camp, who worked in the kitchen, were amazed by the Rebbe's spiritual strength, so much so that they decided to prepare a special kugel for the Rebbe for the next day in honor of Simchas Torah.

When Moshe Eliezer Einhorn brought the kugel to the Rebbe, the Rebbe asked him, "How did they know that today is Simchas Torah?"

Moshe Eliezer answered, "Yesterday when you became upset because you were not excused from work, you said that it was Shemini Atzeres. Who doesn't know that the day after Shemini Atzeres is Simchas Torah?"[9]

In later years, the Rebbe would mention often his experiences on that Shemini Atzeres. With satisfaction evident in his voice, he would say, "True, I was terribly beaten and I barely survived, but in the end I defeated the *reshaim* — I did not go to work on Shemini Atzeres."[10]

---

8 Reported by Yaakov Kahn.
9 Reported by Moshe Eliezer Einhorn.
10 Reported by Yehoshua Veitzenblum.

Chapter 9

Pesach

Food of Faith

As Pesach 1945 approached, the Rebbe began to prepare for the holiday, paying no attention to the chains of his Nazi bondage. With his faith in the Almighty, he did not have even the slightest of concerns as to how he would sustain his body during the eight days of Pesach when he would not eat even the smallest crumb of *chametz*, nor have any benefit from *chametz* — no matter what.

The Rebbe did make an effort to prepare food for Pesach. Together with some fellow prisoners, he gathered a small store of potatoes, hiding them in the cracks of the barracks' walls and between the bunks. But one day the Nazi guards conducted a thorough inspection of the barracks, found the hidden treasures, and confiscated them.

The Rebbe, however, did not worry, relying completely on God. "We have done our part," he said, "and Hashem will do what is good in His eyes."

The Rebbe's followers were astonished when it became clear, the day before Pesach, how correct the Rebbe's approach was. Without any rational explanation or apparent reason, the Nazis suddenly assigned an entire group of Jews to help the farmers whose fields neighbored the camp open up the stores of potatoes which had been underground all winter. Thanks to this work assignment, the Jewish prisoners were able to smuggle back to the camp a large quantity of potatoes.[1]

"We Will Have Matzah"

The Rebbe was firm in his faith in God and announced confidently before Pesach that Heaven would surely assist him to recite the blessing over matzah on the first night of Pesach and to eat at least an olive-size portion of matzah. When a downtrodden Jew cried out painfully, "From where will we get a *kezayis* of matzah for the seder?" the Rebbe calmed him, "You can rest assured that we will have matzah."

Two or three days before Pesach, this Jew came to the Rebbe and asked again, "How will we fulfill the mitzvah of eating matzah?"

The Rebbe replied again in a confident voice: "We will have matzah!"

Moshe Eliezer Einhorn, having overheard this conversation, couldn't help but ask bitterly, "Where will we get matzah from? Will it come down from heaven?"

The Rebbe replied with the same trust in his voice: "You will see, we'll have matzah."[2]

---

1 Reported by Moshe Weiss.
2 Reported by Moshe Eliezer Einhorn.

An Overt Miracle

Then a miracle occurred. That very day, scores of Allied war planes appeared suddenly in the skies and bombed strategic German positions, including the rail station next to the *Waldlager*, which was almost completely destroyed. When the bombing stopped, the Nazis assigned twelve Jewish prisoners to clean up the ruins of the rail station and the train track.

To their joy and surprise, the Jews found a transport of wheat amidst the bombed-out railcars! Hurriedly, they shoveled the grain into their pockets, taking as much as they could carry, knowing that if they were caught they would be severely punished. Despite the risk, they succeeded in smuggling the wheat back into the camp.

The Visheva Rebbe, Rabbi Chaim Yehudah Meir Hager, *zt"l*, was among the Jews assigned to clean up the rail station. "I can't describe the joy that overcame us when we saw the wheat," he related.

In the camp, the prisoners ground the wheat by hand, crushing it with their fingers and small rocks until it was fine enough to be flour. When it came time to bake the matzos, they knew that they were endangering their very lives. If the Germans saw the fire lit in the barracks, every Jew would certainly be killed — any stray spark was interpreted by the Germans as a signal for the enemy bombers and, thus, an act of sabotage.[3]

Secretive Matzah Baking

Late that night, when all the prisoners slept in their bunks, exhausted from the day's work, a few men remained awake,

---

3 Reported by the Visheva Rebbe.

ready to begin their operation. Placing heavy blankets over the windows, they lit a fire in the small metal apparatus which they had prepared for baking the matzos. Outside the door, one of the group stood guard, ready to warn the others to hide everything if the Nazi guards approached. Then the prisoners began mixing the flour with water, kneading the dough, and rolling it out with a rolling pin taken from the camp kitchen. As they worked, they whispered the verses of *Hallel* with a deep intensity. "Praise God! Give praise, you servants of God." Their hearts pounded as they recalled the Sages' interpretation of the words: "We are the servants of God and not the servants of our oppressors."

With the Almighty's help, the matzah baking was completed without incident and a small quantity of kosher matzah was baked. Thus tens of Jews were able to recite the blessing over matzah and perform the mitzvah that seder night.[4]

Among the matzah bakers was a Jew who had converted to Catholicism. During his imprisonment by the Nazis he saw the error of his ways and returned to Judaism, so much so that he volunteered to be the baker in the matzah-baking operation, placing the matzos in the oven and removing them when they were ready.

The Rebbe did not stop this man from serving as the baker, but he would not eat matzos that this former Catholic had baked. In the short time that was left before the onset of the holiday, the Rebbe, with the help of one of his followers, baked a few small matzos for himself, each the volume of an olive, so that he would have enough for the seder.[5]

---

4 See note above.
5 Reported by Moshe Weiss.

A Night as Bright as Day

When the holiday began, several dozen Sanzer and Vizhnitzer chassidim gathered for *maariv* in the barracks of Rabbi Meir Hershkowitz, who had been appointed barracks leader of one of the Muldorf barracks. The Rebbe was asked to be the chazzan. As was his way, he wept and davened for a long time, seemingly oblivious to the fear that surrounded him. One of the prisoners stood watch at the barracks door to make sure that the Germans did not approach.

After davening, the prisoners dispersed, except for approximately fifteen men who remained to participate in the seder. The Klausenberger Rebbe sat at the head of the table, and to his right was the Visheva Rebbe. To his left sat Rabbi Aharon Teitelbaum, *av beis din* of Nyirbator, and Rabbi Yehudah Gottlieb, *av beis din* of Miskolc.

The Klausenberger Rebbe recited the entire Haggadah from memory. His cries shook the rest of the prisoners, who listened with tears streaming down their faces. Of course, they did not have the four cups of wine. They ate bitter herbs every day. Only in the eating of the matzah did they find pleasure and joy, like people who had discovered a great treasure.

The Rebbe spoke words of encouragement and chassidic teachings. Anyone who listened to him could not help but be amazed at how he retained a clarity of mind that allowed him to serve God at the highest level even under the hellish conditions of Nazi terror. When others were afflicted by depression and mental disorientation, the Rebbe's thoughts were consumed with spiritual matters and ideas about which no one else could think.[6]

6 This entire seder was described by Moshe Weiss.

Reb Meir Hershkowitz, the barracks leader, had invited to the seder the barracks leader from the neighboring barracks, an irreligious Polish Jew who knew nothing about Judaism. He sat silently throughout the seder, watching everything that was taking place without uttering a sound. Then, suddenly, he stood up, unable to contain himself any longer. "Jewish brothers! If I had not seen this beautiful scene with my own eyes I would not have believed that such a thing was possible...that Jews should observe the commandment of eating matzah under the noses of the German murderers, with death staring at them in the face. I would never have believed it."[7]

Surviving the Week of Pesach

Avraham Eidels, one of the Rebbe's followers, related, During Pesach the Rebbe hardly ate anything. He refused to even touch the stale bread that was distributed daily to the prisoners, unlike others who, to save their lives, traded their portion of bread for vegetables and other foods that were not *chametz*. The Rebbe left his portion of bread unclaimed; anyone who wanted it could take it. All he would eat were unpeeled potatoes which someone was occasionally able to obtain for him. He baked them in an empty can that he had made kosher in boiling water before Pesach.

"I remember that on the last day of Pesach, the Rebbe did not have his can with him because he had been sent out on a work detail outside the camp grounds. He refused to eat a baked potato that someone offered him because it had been cooked in a dish that had not been made kosher for Pesach. As he was

---

7 Reported by the Visheva Rebbe.

working, the Rebbe found the head of a sugar beet. His face shone with happiness at this discovery, especially as it came on the heels of withstanding the test of the baked potato. As he ate it, he remarked, 'I have never tasted anything as sweet as this.' "

Yaakov Kahn, who was sixteen years old at the time, was encouraged by the Rebbe not to eat any *chametz* that Pesach. Together with a friend, he decided to undertake the mitzvah. "On the last day of the holiday," he related, "we were extremely weak and could not go hungry anymore. We desperately wanted to eat some bread. But when the Rebbe saw that we were wavering, he encouraged us some more. 'If you have remained strong this long, most of the *yom tov*, please put in just a little bit more effort to complete the day. I promise that you will not die!'

"The force of his holy words burned like a fire and we decided not to eat the bread. Later that day a miracle occurred. A kitchen worker came up to us out of nowhere with a hat full of potatoes that had been baked in their skins, which he gave to my friend and me!"

Redemption Is Near

The day after Pesach, after having survived the entire holiday on almost no food, the Rebbe approached a young kitchen worker, Yaakov Eliezer Dirnfeld, and asked if he could bring him some food, perhaps a carrot or a potato. He was so weak, he told the young boy, that he felt all his energy ebbing away.

"My heart tells me," he added quietly, "that our redemption is very near. It would be terrible if I was not able to remain strong in my vow not to eat forbidden foods until the end. I have been so careful throughout all these terrible days not to eat even a crumb of nonkosher food."

Despite the great danger, Yaakov Eliezer took some vegetables and other kosher food from the kitchen storeroom and gave them to the Rebbe so that he could regain his strength.

Three weeks later, the American army reached Muldorf and liberated the prisoners.[8]

8 Reported by Yaakov Eliezer Dirnfeld.

Chapter 10

An End to the Darkness

The Nazis' Death Throes

The Germans realized that their end was near. However, because the gas chambers and crematoria in Dachau had not been in use for several months, they had to look for other ways to make the most of their final days in control.

Shortly after Pesach, the remnants of Muldorf's inmates were taken on a cruel death march which lasted many days. They were forced to run from place to place, without rhyme or reason, and with no food or rest. Occasionally, they were put on railcars and transported a short distance back and forth, enough time for rumors to spread among the prisoners that they were being taken to the mountains on the Austrian border to be killed. Many Jews were killed by various means during these final days.

The False Liberation

On Friday, April 27 (14 Iyar), a strange event took place, which was afterwards referred to as the "false liberation." When the train made a stop in a small village, some SS officers burst into the railcars and announced, "You are free!" With dramatic gestures, they tore their *Wehrmacht* emblems off their uniforms.

Many of the prisoners believed the announcement and hurriedly got off the train, running in every direction to look for food and other necessities. The Rebbe, however, immediately turned to the people around him and asked, "Today is *erev Shabbos*. Where will we go?" In the same breath he whispered, "My heart tells me that not everything here is as it should be."

He suggested that all remain for the moment in the cars. Only some of the men took his advice.

Suddenly and without warning, SS troops on bicycles appeared from all directions, machine guns in their hands, firing everywhere and killing hundreds. At the same time, American airplanes began dropping bombs everywhere, killing many innocent people. Only the Rebbe and those who stayed with him on the train because of Shabbos remained alive and uninjured.

Then it was quiet. The shooting stopped. Darkness fell. Shabbos came. The men in the railcars were stunned by the day's events, bewildered and confused. Only the Rebbe was able to think clearly. He had one and only one concern at that moment: How could he fulfill the mitzvah of eating the Shabbos meals?

Preparing the King's Feast

The Rebbe went from car to car, seeking someone who had a bit of extra food. "Who wants to acquire a place in the World to Come?" he asked. "Who can give me something to eat in honor of Shabbos?"

Finally, he came upon Yaakov Kahn, who had hidden some

raw potatoes under his shirt. The boy winked at the Rebbe, indicating that he was willing to give him some of his hidden treasure later, when the other prisoners had gone to sleep, so that no one else would see.

The Rebbe returned a few hours later, and Yaakov handed the Rebbe a raw potato. Immediately, the Rebbe began to sing with great excitement and intensity, "*Askinu se'udasa*..... I shall prepare the feast of perfect faith.... I shall prepare the feast of the King." With this one raw potato, the Rebbe fulfilled the mitzvah of the Shabbos meal as if he were sitting at a table full of delicacies.

When he finished eating, he turned to the young boy shyly. "Am I correct that you have some more? You look to me to be unusually rounded. Maybe you can give me another potato for the 'feast of the Ancient One'?" Yaakov agreed and gave the Rebbe another potato for the next Shabbos meal.

The Rebbe was overjoyed. "I am not going to say thank you — I won't even think about how to return the favor because I want the Repayer of all kindness to reward you Himself. You cannot fathom what you have done for me this Shabbos. Without you I would not have been able to fulfill the mitzvah of eating the Shabbos meals."[1]

The Real Liberation

Two days later, on Monday, April 30 (17 Iyar), the Muldorf *Waldlager* prisoners finally experienced the moment that they had been longing for: liberation. The Nazis transported them by train back and forth, back and forth, several times until they

---

1 Reported by Yaakov Kahn.

stopped suddenly near the village of Tunesig, got off the train, and disappeared.

The prisoners approached the openings of the railcars to see what had happened. They were stunned to see American soldiers spread out on the road beneath the rail bridge. Within seconds the soldiers had climbed onto the train and approached the prisoners' cars with smiles and happy cries, throwing packages of chocolate and candy to the prisoners. Only then did the prisoners understand that they were really free.

From Death to Life

"*Baruch Hashem*, we have been saved!" were the Rebbe's first words upon learning of his liberation.[2] Still standing in the railcar, the Rebbe immediately grasped the significance of what was taking place. "If the Master of the Universe in His great compassion and mercy has saved me from death, I am obligated to dedicate my life, from this moment onward, to Him and His honor, for it is forbidden to derive personal pleasure from miracles."

Standing next to him, unable to fully absorb what was happening, were several of his followers, including Eliezer Hager, Eliyahu Yaakov Steinmetz, and Hershel Lax. They stood bewildered, like a person emerging from a dark room and being blinded by the bright light outside.

An American army officer climbed into the railcar and announced excitedly, "You are now under the protection of the United States Army. Soon our people will come take care of you and give you food. You will be taken to a safe location and will

---

2 Reported by Eliyahu Yaakov Steinmetz.

have everything that you need."

The survivors gathered around him, staring at him with empty, despondent eyes. They could not grasp what he was trying to tell them. "Are these hellish days really over?"

A Request for Kosher Food

Suddenly, the Rebbe pushed his way through the crowd to the officer. "With all due respect," he began, "it is important that you know that some of the people here are Jewish, and they can eat only kosher food. We will be forever grateful to your army if you provide us with food we can eat."

Hearing the Rebbe's request, some of the survivors, who had been mentally and emotionally affected by the torture, screamed, "There he goes again, starting his *mishegas*. Who needs kosher food now?!"

The Rebbe turned to them calmly and explained with great patience, "Please understand, my beloved brothers, the atrocities have ended. We are going to return to normal life now. We are Jews, and we are obligated to eat only kosher food."

To his followers, who surrounded him like sheep around a shepherd, the Rebbe repeated, "We must not forget that we are Jews. A Jew can eat only kosher food."[3]

Shortly thereafter, the Red Cross arrived with huge amounts of food. The non-Jewish Muldorf survivors had enjoyed special privileges in the *Waldlager* and were strong enough to pounce on the food and grab large portions. The Jews, however, were so weak that by the time they dragged themselves to the place where the food was being distributed, there was al-

3 Reported by Yaakov Yitzchak Berminka.

most nothing left. The Rebbe and his followers, however, did not move an inch. Despite their weakened state, they did not take any of the food.[4]

A Jewish American soldier passed the railcar and saw that the Rebbe trying to get his attention. "What can I do for you?" he asked with concern.

The Rebbe pointed to his head. "A yarmulke!"[5]

"Shehakol Nihiyeh Bidvaro"

The Rebbe's presence of mind in those first hours of freedom are also illustrated by the following story, which he related to his relative, Rabbi Shmuel Unsdorfer. During the Rebbe's nine months of imprisonment in Muldorf, he could often see a stream of clear water which flowed on the other side of the camp's fence. But the fence was electrified and he could not go near it.

The Rebbe frequently prayed, "Have mercy on me, merciful Father, and allow to immerse myself in a purifying spring just one more time in my life. Have mercy on me and allow me to recite the blessing of *Shehakol* on its fresh water just one more time."

As soon as the Rebbe was able, he hurried to the forest stream and leaped into its water to ritually immerse himself. After reciting the blessing *Shehakol Nihiyeh Bidvaro* with great emotion, in a way he had never done before, the Rebbe took a drink of the crystal-clear liquid.

Later, when he related the story, the Rebbe said, "If only I

4 Reported by Moshe Weiss.
5 Reported by Rabbi S. Fried.

could say the blessing of *Shehakol* like that again."[6]

When the Rebbe emerged from the stream, he cried out with joy, "All these days, I was afraid that it was decreed that I should die without immersion. Now that I have finally merited to immerse myself, I am no longer afraid of anything in the world...except for Hashem and His greatness."[7]

Entering the DP Camp

After a short time, the survivors were told to get off the train for some fresh air. They were directed to a nearby field, where they stayed for two days, sleeping under the sky. Then they were transferred via military motorcade to a displaced persons camp in Feldafing, near Munich, in the area under American control.

The camp had previously been the campus of a Hitler Youth school. Immediately upon finding the trainful of Nazi prisoners, the Americans converted it into a camp for displaced persons, which quickly became known as a "DP camp." It was clearly heavenly intervention which turned this former Hitler Youth school into the first center for the renewal of Jewish life after the Holocaust.

The frightened and dazed Jews brought to Feldafing were greeted at the camp entrance by a staff of supervisors and army workers, who handed out loaves of bread, pajamas, and under-clothing. They asked the survivors to remove their torn prisoners' uniforms so they could be burned for hygienic purposes.

As night fell that Wednesday, May 2 (19 Iyar), the survivors were temporarily housed in the camp's "white houses," under

---

6 Reported by Rabbi Shmuel Unsdorfer.
7 Reported by Avraham Eidels.

relatively decent conditions, and given medical care. The German kitchen staff, which had previously cooked for Hitler Youth and was now under the control of the American forces, was ordered to continue operating the kitchen as it had before for the camp's new residents.

"Choose Life"

The Jewish survivors brought to the DP camp were mere skeletons, in a state of complete physical deterioration. Many who had held their own during the years of Nazi oppression now collapsed upon liberation. Some died, others broke down, and yet others fell into deep depression and lost the will to live. More than a few declared that they would have been better off dying in a gas chamber.

In those first few difficult days, the Rebbe stood up. A survivor among survivors, his lips trembled from weakness and suffering. He too was skin and bones, but his eyes shone brightly with an extraordinary light as he announced, "We are alive because we are Jews and we were commanded by Hashem to 'choose life.' It is written in our holy Torah, 'You who cling to Hashem, your God, You are alive today.' "

At that moment, the Rebbe's superhuman leadership abilities were ignited within him. It appeared to others that a divine spirit rested upon him. In a split second he became the leader and spokesman for all the downtrodden survivors living in the DP camp, and he did not hesitate to tell them what the Almighty expected of them in this unusual time.

The Rebbe approached his mission with great courage and with extraordinary self-restraint in the face of his own enor-

mous personal tragedy. His soul directed him to arise and ac-
tively pursue the mitzvah of choosing life and to enable his fellow Jews to do the same. From the innermost recesses of his
soul and the depths of his heart came a supernatural strength
which were needed to rebuild life from among the heaps of ash
and embers.

And life to the Rebbe meant — of course — a Jewish life.

Burying the Dead

The Rebbe's first priority was to bury the dead. The area
surrounding the camp and the train tracks was littered with the
corpses of Jews who had either been killed by the Nazis or died
of starvation. The Rebbe had seen these corpses from the train,
but at that time there had been no way for him to bury them.

Now he quickly approached the DP camp commanders and
requested that a car and driver be assigned to him for the purpose of collecting the corpses. He organized a group of five or
six young survivors to join him in searching for the dead and
bringing them to the area set aside for burial.

The Rebbe supervised this effort personally. It lasted for
several weeks and involved great danger, but this did not deter
him. He established a burial society and appointed Rabbi
Yechezkel Rutner, the former rabbi of Shamkot, at its head. The
Rebbe also assisted in preparing the dead for burial and in dig-
ging the graves. He instructed that Kaddish be recited for each
person buried.

This effort was physically very difficult for the Rebbe and
the survivors who assisted him. They all became infected with
typhus as a result of handling the corpses. Nonetheless, the

Rebbe insisted that it was obligatory to bury the dead without delay.[8] Besides the mitzvah involved, perhaps the Rebbe also wanted to demonstrate to the survivors that they were alive and that the time had come once again to distinguish between the living and the dead.

Reestablishing the Concept of Kosher Food

The Rebbe also reminded those around him of the concept of kashrus, an idea that had been completely forgotten during the Holocaust. The Rebbe's followers relate that during the first days after liberation, when they were still physically weak and run down, the Rebbe did not stop anyone from eating from the camp kitchen because other sources of food did not exist. Most ate whatever they could get and the Rebbe did not criticize them because saving their lives was paramount. Even those who asked the Rebbe whether it was permissible to eat the milk and cheese produced by non-Jews were told that at that time it was permissible. Later, however, the Rebbe spoke publicly about the need to observe kashrus and announced that it was now time to refrain from eating non-Jewish milk products, except for butter (since butter cannot be made from nonkosher milk).[9]

The Rebbe, having been extremely careful to eat only kosher food during the period of his imprisonment, continued his strict adherence to kashrus despite his weak state. Survivor Baruch Ganz recalled, "I lived two barracks away from the Rebbe [in Feldafing]. Two days after liberation, the Rebbe returned to his barracks exhausted and drained from searching

8 Reported by Moshe Weiss.
9 Reported by David Greenzweig.

for the dead, and I was worried about what he would eat. I knew he had not eaten anything all day.

"A young Jewish teenager entered the barracks and I saw him empty a can of preserves. I eagerly took the empty can, boiled water in it, and prepared a cup of tea for the Rebbe. Then I walked over to the Rebbe's barracks, Barracks A.

"I found the Rebbe lying on a bag of straw on the cold floor. He was literally at the end of his strength. When he saw that I held the cup in my hand, he asked me, 'What did you bring?'

" 'A cup of tea,' I answered.

"I was sure that he would drink it quickly to rejuvenate himself. But the Rebbe asked me in his weak voice, 'What did you boil the water in?'

"I told him the truth, that I had boiled the water in an empty can of preserves. Without any hesitation, he responded, 'If so, put it aside. I will not drink it.' He was concerned because the can had not been made kosher or immersed in a *mikveh*."

Establishing a Kosher Kitchen in the Camp

The Rebbe's personal example had a deep impression on young Baruch. He asked himself, "What about me? Now that I have been saved, should I also continue eating *treif*?" Baruch approached two of his friends and convinced them to also stop eating nonkosher. Together, the three went to an UNRWA official with the request, "We want only dry foods, uncooked, nothing from the kitchen!"

When the official did not respond quickly enough, they went to the camp storage facility and secretly traded cigarettes for some dry foods. The news of the trade spread throughout the camp, and soon some twenty other survivors, mostly youth, wanted to eat only kosher food. The group appointed a delegation that went to ask the Rebbe for assistance.

Immediately upon receiving this request, the Rebbe decided to establish a kosher kitchen in the camp to provide meals for any survivor who asked, in particular for the youth. He appointed Baruch Ganz to run the technical aspects of the kitchen, while the Rebbe himself tried to obtain the necessary equipment and finances from the camp management.[10]

At first, a makeshift kitchen was opened. On an open road in the heart of the camp, without any appliances to speak of, a large barrel was set up, a fire was lit, and the cooking began. Initially the cooking food was limited to pareve foods only. Given the conditions, perhaps the quality of the food was less than ideal, but without any doubt, the establishment of the kitchen represented the first step in the renewal of the observance of kashrus among the survivors. Soon, upon the Rebbe's initiative, tens of other public kosher kitchens which fed thousands of survivors were opened in all of the DP camps throughout Germany.

Aharon Baron, who spent several months with the Rebbe in the Muldorf *Waldlager* and later in Feldafing, recalled, "It is impossible to describe in simple words the enormity of the Rebbe's efforts to set up a kosher public kitchen for us. Today, it is difficult to fully understand its significance. But at that time, people had forgotten how to conduct themselves, not just as Jews, but as rational human beings. The Rebbe, however, knew exactly what he had to do at that time."

---

10 Reported by Baruch Ganz.

Tefillin with a Blessing

When the Rebbe discovered that among the American officers was a religious Jewish officer, Lieutenant Meyer Birnbaum, he asked him whether he had a pair of kosher tefillin. The officer responded that he had a beautiful pair of tefillin that had been written by a very pious chassidic scribe.

The Rebbe's eyes lit up. Emotionally, he explained, "*Baruch Hashem*! This is the first time in a very long time that I have found tefillin that can be worn with a blessing. Up to now, under the Nazi oppression, even when I was able to find a pair of tefillin I never knew if they were really kosher, and so I would put them on without a blessing. But now...."

It did not take long for the news about the tefillin to spread among the survivors. All the Rebbe's barracks-mates longed to put the tefillin on themselves. From that day forward men would line up to perform the mitzvah of tefillin under the watchful eye of the Rebbe, who insisted that no one wear the tefillin too long. He would say, "Say the blessing, put the tefillin on your arm and head, say the Shema. Now please take them off and quickly wind them up so that the next person in line can have a turn."[11]

---

11 Meyer Birnbaum with Yonason Rosenblum, *Lieutenant Birnbaum: A Soldier's Story* (New York: Mesorah Publications, 1993), p. 155.

Chapter 11

The First Shabbos after Liberation

Preparing a Beis Midrash

Three days after liberation, the Rebbe began to prepare for Shabbos. He gathered several teenage boys and asked them to help set up a synagogue and *beis midrash* for the survivors. In exchange, the Rebbe promised them that as soon as he obtained tefillin they would be among the first to put them on.[1]

The boys excitedly joined the Rebbe in a careful survey of all the camp buildings for an appropriate available building. After a thorough search, they found a large, spacious, empty hall which had previously been used as a music hall for the Hitler Youth. The hall was perfect for a *beis midrash*. The Rebbe obtained permission from the camp officials to use the building, while the boys went through the camp announcing that the *beis midrash* would be opened and that they would be praying there that very night.

---

1 Reported by David Greenzweig.

The announcement was greeted with great excitement. Under the Rebbe's supervision, the boys cleaned up the hall and prepared it for prayer. They brought in some benches and a few tables and prepared paper yarmulkes for the survivors. For the Rebbe, who was still wearing a striped prisoner uniform, the boys found a short military *Wehrmacht* uniform. On his head he wore a boat-shaped Hitler Youth hat. On his feet he wore wooden clogs.

The Rebbe, whose beard had began to grow anew, was filled with excitement that entire Friday. After immersing himself in a spring in honor of Shabbos, he asked for suggestions on how to obtain a tallis. He was given a sheet from the camp warehouse which he could use. The Rebbe found a spool of wool, which he spun by hand into strings for tzitzis. The spinning was very difficult and took many hours. In the end, the Rebbe did not have enough time properly to tie the knots on the strings and had to make do with just the first knots.

Approaching the Creator

At *minchah* time, the music hall filled with hundreds of Jews — everyone in the camp who wanted to remember that he was Jewish. The Rebbe wrapped himself in his makeshift tallis and went to the front of the room to lead the services. He began to recite the Friday afternoon *minchah* service in a heartbreaking voice. "Give thanks to God for He is good; His kindness endures forever!"

The congregation of survivors stood there and cried. None of them had siddurim, but it didn't matter. The Rebbe was extremely weak and his voice trembled, yet with every moment it grew louder and louder until it filled the large room and pierced the heavens above: "Say those redeemed by God, who saved them from the enemy."

With more cries and greater intensity the Rebbe continued, "Children of Man, who sit in darkness and the shadow of death, shackled in affliction and iron. He removed them from darkness and the shadow of death, and broke open their shackles. The fools — because of their sinful path and their iniquities they were afflicted. Their soul abhorred all food, and they reached from the portals of death." From the depths of his heart he cried out, "Then they cried out to Hashem in their distress."

The foundations of the hall shook as the survivors cried with the Rebbe. Their davening lasted over an hour and a half.[2]

"I Have Kindled My Bed"

After davening, the Rebbe sat down to eat his meal with a number of fellow survivors, including Rabbi Yehudah Gottlieb, the rabbi of Miskolc, and Reb Moshe Hoffman of Papa, among others.

After singing *Shalom Aleichem* in the well-known Sanz melody, the Rebbe recited the prayer *Ribbon Kol HaOlamim* in a most moving and surprising fashion. When he reached the phrase "Allow us the merit to receive Shabbos amid abundant gladness," the Rebbe became very emotional and drew out the words at length. When he came to the words, "For I have kindled my lights and made my bed," he let out a wail and reversed the words, saying, "For I have kindled my bed and made my lights," just as his grandfather the Divrei Chaim had done the

2 Reported by David Greenzweig.

Shabbos before his death. Over and over again the Rebbe repeated these words, not only on the first Friday night after liberation but also on many Friday nights that followed.

The Rebbe recited Kiddush over two pieces of black bread in lieu of challah loaves. His entire meal consisted of a few potatoes which had been cooked specially for him in a can that had been properly made kosher. Afterwards, he gave a Torah discourse centering around their situation. "We never imagined that it would end this way, with the surrender of the cursed Germans," he said. "We hoped that not even a leaf would survive in this land of murder and evil."[3] "Was this what we had hoped for? American soldiers? We had hoped for *shivtei Kah*!"

Later, the Rebbe was asked why he had said that he had been hoping to be rescued by the *shivtei Kah*, the tribes of the Almighty, and not by Mashiach. He responded, "The *Yismach Moshe* explains that the verse 'The saviors will ascend Mount Zion' is a reference to those Jews who were exiled across the Sambatyon River. I, too, was referring to these saviors and to the final redemption."[4]

Shabbos Day

The next day, after an impassioned and moving prayer service that lasted for hours, the Rebbe sat down at a table outside the makeshift *beis midrash*, an onion in hand, and began to sing, "*Chai Hashem U'Varuch Tzuri.*" Immediately he was surrounded by hundreds of Jews, many of whom were still far from observance, whose hearts were stirred by his melody.

---

3 Reported by Yaakov Eliezer Dirnfeld.
4 Reported by Mordechai Weber.

At this meal, too, the Rebbe gave a Torah discourse, this time trying to strengthen and encourage his broken and suffering fellow survivors. Surely, he said, the Master of the Universe would avenge the blood of His people. Just as the Nazis had executed their evil plans with German precision, so Hashem would repay them in kind with great precision and detailed plans — measure for measure. "The verse says, 'To execute upon them written judgment,' " the Rebbe exclaimed. "He will impose upon them not just any judgment, but rather a written judgment, one of revenge precisely crafted."[5]

In the afternoon, all kinds of people gathered around the Rebbe, including some irreligious Jewish partisans. The Rebbe discussed original ideas and thoughts about the role and destiny of the Jewish people. Speaking for close to two hours, he quoted from memory full sections from different *sefarim*, as if the books were open in front of him. Those who had never met the Rebbe applauded in amazement and commented, "He is so learned and scholarly and knowledgeable in world affairs. Obviously, he is extremely well read."[6]

During the third Shabbos meal the Rebbe spoke at great length, enthusiastically expounding on lofty spiritual ideas as though he were speaking directly to the heavens. He did not care whether anyone was listening. This had been his custom even in Auschwitz. He never missed speaking words of Torah during *seudah shelishis*, even when he talked only to himself, his face afire and his eyes closed.

---

5 Reported by Chaim Alter Rota.
6 Reported by David Greenzweig.

Chapter 12

Gathering Up the Exiles

Searching for Fellow Survivors

After Shabbos, the Rebbe again turned his attention to gathering up the dead for burial. His search, however, was not limited to looking for the dead. In the vehicle that the Americans assigned to his use, he traveled to all the towns around Feldafing with the motto "I am searching for my brothers."

Scattered throughout the area were Jews who had survived the war by hiding in attics and underground bunkers. Having been out of touch with the outside world for such a long time, they thought that Hitler had exterminated the entire Jewish people and that they were the only survivors, with no hope of ever resuming Jewish lives.

Knowing this, the Rebbe traveled to a different town each day. He would go to the center of town and speak to the villagers as though he was curious about their situation. In the course of the conversation he would mention the Jews, and sometimes a villager would say casually, "There is a Jewish survivor in so-and-so's house."

The Rebbe followed every lead in the hopes of finding a forgotten Jew hidden by the gentiles. When he found such a Jew, he did his utmost to convince him to leave his hiding place and come to the DP camp, where there were many Jews.[1]

The Rebbe's Powers of Persuasion

Many of these survivors followed the Rebbe to Feldafing without any real desire to go. They were comfortable where they were. The Americans provided food and support for refugees wherever they were, even those who lived among non-Jews by choice. No one was being pushed at that time to find a job and establish himself. The Rebbe, however, used all his powers of persuasion to convince these survivors to return to their brethren.

The survivors were still confused and shaken by all that they had gone through. Some said openly that after all they had gone through they had no desire to live as Jews anymore. The Rebbe, however, knew how to respond to these protests. He had no intention of asking them to do any such thing, he would tell them. His only concern was for their physical well-being — that they not be left to rely upon the kindness of non-Jews. "Isn't it better to be among your own flesh and blood?" he would ask them.[2]

Once the Rebbe encouraged a young Jewish teenager to come to the DP camp. The boy resisted because he was sure the Rebbe would not let him go to movies. The Rebbe, however, promised the boy that when life returned to normal and a movie

---

1 Reported by Moshe Weiss.
2 See note above.

theater was opened for the survivors he would give him money to see a show. With this assurance in hand, the teenager joined the Rebbe. Not too long after that a movie theater was opened, and the Rebbe kept his promise. Eventually, this young boy did *teshuvah* and returned to Torah observance.[3]

Meir Shraga Perdelsky, who was with the Rebbe in the *Waldlager*, recalled, "Until the last day in the concentration camp I firmly believed that the final redemption was near, largely as a result of the Rebbe's influence. When my dreams did not materialize and Mashiach did not arrive, the Rebbe and I went our separate ways.

"When I arrived at Feldafing I went to see the Rebbe. He understood my inner struggle, but did not lecture me. His only request was that I join him as his guest for the upcoming high holidays. When I came to him on *erev Yom Kippur* for a blessing, he blessed me and added, 'Be yourself.' "

This is how the Rebbe succeeded in bringing to Feldafing hundreds of lost Jews whose inner spark of holiness was rekindled as a result of his efforts. Eventually, over time, these Jews returned to their faith and became faithful and observant Jews. Most built beautiful, Torah-true homes and raised families of proud Jews.

A Mother's Comfort

Like a mother, the Rebbe comforted the downtrodden and broken Jews around him, even though he was in the same situation as they and he should have been equally as needy. It did not make any difference to the Rebbe whether a Jew was from Hun-

---

3 Reported by the boy himself.

gary or from Russia, Poland, or Lithuania, a chassid or *misnaged*. "If you are a Jew, you are my brother! I will do everything that I can for you!" the Rebbe would say.

Overflowing with compassion and understanding, the Rebbe spoke with each survivor in gentle and pleasant tones. "You are alive!" he would say to them. He was able to find just the right way to talk to every individual. Chaim Alter Rota recalled, "At the same time that the Rebbe told one survivor, 'Even though none of our loved ones have survived, HaKadosh Baruch Hu is still alive and exists among us!' he would tell another, 'You will see. The world will return to normal and you will return to business and commerce.' " Precisely with these words, which at the time sounded almost ludicrous, the Rebbe was able to draw the person out of his depression.

Spiritual Crisis

To fully comprehend the import of the Rebbe's actions, one must understand the emotional and mental condition of the newly liberated survivors. They were broken and shattered in both body and soul. The long period of imprisonment and torture in the concentration camps had left them with deep wounds that would never fully heal. During the Nazi oppression, they had suppressed all emotion and thought — there was no time to think about their parents, their children, and other lost family members. After liberation, however, they were forced to confront the destruction and their personal loss. Overcome with hopelessness, they felt that their lots were worse than Iyov's.

The awareness that the world had been completely indifferent to their tragedy and the civilized nations had stood idly by as the Nazis systematically exterminated European Jewry and subjected its remnants to inhuman suffering also contributed to the survivors' despair. Additionally, the survivors suffered from various contagious diseases that spread among them and caused many deaths. The DP camp was enveloped in total despair and spiritual despondency. Even those who had been able to maintain their equilibrium and connection to religion during the years of the Nazi oppression were now collapsing.

The spiritual crisis affected virtually every survivor. It was incredibly difficult just to withstand the stress, let alone to view their situations as a test of faith, a decree from heaven to be lovingly accepted. It was even more difficult to believe in the eternal nature and inherent holiness of the Jewish people, especially since the camp was full of antireligious Jews who took advantage of the situation and attempted to eradicate Torah and faith in God from the Jewish people.

A Light for the Masses

Precisely during that very dark period, the Klausenberger Rebbe illuminated the world for his fellow survivors. At that critical time, the survivors desperately needed an extraordinary spiritual leader — one of their own, someone who had himself experienced the Nazi hell yet whose spirit was unbroken. By personal example, the Rebbe demonstrated that one could remain close to his Creator despite all that had occurred and actually grow stronger in faith through the suffering.

There were many observant Jews among the survivors, including many rabbis and Torah scholars, who had withstood the trials and tribulations of the Nazi persecution with their faith in the Almighty intact and encouraged others to observe the mitzvos. But in order to have a major impact on the masses of survivors, a spiritual giant, head and shoulders above the rest, was required. Only the Klausenberger Rebbe was able to overcome the spiritual despair that had overtaken the survivors.

Overcoming his own personal agony and feelings of despair by drawing upon an enormous reservoir of inner strength, the Rebbe became a living example of faith and spiritual fortitude. Survivors who knew him were unable to comprehend how he was able to accept so much suffering without even a hint of complaint. Those who harbored complaints against God either because of their own horrendous experiences or because of the mass destruction and killing which He had sanctioned were left speechless when they learned of the Rebbe's situation.

After losing his entire family in the Holocaust — his mother, his wife, and ten of his children — the Rebbe learned that his eldest son, Lipele, had survived the concentration camps and was in a DP camp near Feldafing for a short time. He succumbed to illness before the Rebbe heard that he had survived.

The Rebbe was in the hospital when he received the news of his son's death. He rose from his sickbed, recited the full blessing *Baruch Dayan HaEmes* with great emotion, and announced in a voice that could be heard from one end of the hospital to the other that he did not harbor, God forbid, any complaints against Hashem's judgment and that he accepted all of His decrees with love.[4]

(The Rebbe later told his followers that he had put much ef-

4 Reported by Chaim Alter Rota in *Dos Yiddishe Vort* 253 (New York: Iyar/Sivan 1985), p. 38–39.

fort into not falling into depression of any sort. One day in Feldafing, however, he suddenly felt a twinge of pain in his heart without knowing what caused it. Later, when he was informed of his son Lipele's passing, he realized that the pain had come on the same day that Lipele had died. His heart had been aware of the tragedy.[5])

On His Sickbed

After two and a half weeks of strenuous rescue efforts, the Rebbe took sick with typhus, which had broken out in deathly proportions among the survivors in Feldafing. His weakened physical state, the extremely poor hygienic conditions, and the Rebbe's exposure to the killer disease for several days while helping others who were sick all contributed to the Rebbe's contraction of the illness. On Shavuos he collapsed with a very high fever. On the second day of the holiday, which was Shabbos, the camp doctors rushed him to the hospital in critical condition.

Typhus took the lives of many residents of Feldafing because they lacked the strength to fight it. The Rebbe lay on his sickbed for close to three months, hovering between life and death. As he would later describe it, he felt as if his fingertips were being pricked by thousands of needles.[6] His eyesight was so affected by the terrible disease that he could barely read.

Some of the medical staff lost hope and stopped treating him. When the camp commander, Colonel Smith, came to check on the Rebbe and discovered this, he gave stern orders to do everything possible to save the Rebbe. Otherwise, he told the

---

5 Reported by Moshe Weiss.
6 Reported by Yehoshua Veitzenblum.

medical staff, he would hold them personally accountable for his death.[7]

The doctors consulted among themselves and informed the Rebbe that he had to greatly increase his food and drink intake. But the Rebbe refused to even touch food which came from the camp kitchen. Several other rabbis in the infirmary, including Reb Moshe Schwartz from Kleinwardein and Rabbi Moshe Aryeh Halberstam, pleaded with the Rebbe to eat, but to no avail. Even when the American army distributed care packages full of food, the Rebbe did not touch his and left it for the other patients in the room.[8] Only when the Rebbe was brought some cereal that had been cooked in the kosher kitchen he had established did he eat.[9]

In his book *Zechor V'Al Tishkach*, Yirmiyah Tessler writes, "I learned that the great tzaddik Rabbi Yekusiel Yehudah Halberstam was in Feldafing…. When I arrived there I found the Rebbe critically ill with typhus…. As soon as I entered the room, the Rebbe blessed me with the blessing of *Shehechiyanu*, including God's name. Tears ran down my face and I cried bitterly, seeing the great rabbi of our city in such critical condition, but at the same time I was comforted by the fact that the Almighty had saved his soul from the Nazis."[10]

In the Presence of the Divine

Eliyahu Reisman, a survivor who spent three months in the

---

7 Reported by Yaakov Yitzchak Berminka.
8 Reported by Yehoshua Veitzenblum.
9 Reported by Yaakov Yitzchak Berminka, whose wife worked in the kosher kitchen and personally prepared food for the Rebbe.
10 Tessler, p. 122.

Feldafing hospital, recalled, "I was admitted to the hospital a few days after Shavuos, unconscious and running a very high fever. After several days I regained consciousness and saw that I was lying right next to the Rebbe. I was encouraged by the fact that the Rebbe was at my side, even though his condition was very critical. I thought to myself, *If the Shechinah rests above every sick person then all the more so above the Klausenberger Rebbe!* This feeling gave me strength.

"I was a teenager at the time, an orphan, alone in the world. The Rebbe lent me his tefillin every day. When he began to recover, he would rise from his bed on Shabbos, especially in the afternoon for the third meal, and conduct a small *tisch* in our room, complete with words of Torah and *zemiros*.

"The Rebbe made a great impression upon me. He never lost his focus even for a moment and was always devoted to Hashem. I was especially awed by his strong desire to learn. Someone once brought him a few *sefarim* which had been which been buried in the Munich cemetery during the war. Although the Rebbe's eyesight was very poor because of his illness, he would pick up a *sefer* and bring it right up to his eyes to try to read it.

"Since he was so weak, the Rebbe was not able to concentrate on highly complex topics. He therefore asked for a *chumash* and began to diligently review the entire year's worth of Torah readings with the Targum in order to make up for those he had missed during his imprisonment.

"The Rebbe amazed us all when one day the rabbi of Shamkot, Rabbi Yechezkel Rutner, came to see him. Reb Yechezkel related that he had been asked to perform a marriage ceremony in the camp but did not have a proper *kesubah* nor a text to which he could refer in order to write one. Although the Rebbe was suffering from a very high fever, he proceeded to dictate the entire *kesubah* text to him from memory."

Chapter 13

Returning His Brethren to Observance

Leaving the Hospital

As he began to regain his strength, the Rebbe once again began to circulate among the survivors. Although he was still weak and could walk only short distances and then only by leaning on a wall, he left his bed to care for his beloved brethren.

The first thing on the Rebbe's agenda was kosher food. He told all whom he met that they must stop eating nonkosher food. The time had come to gather together and demand a kosher kitchen for the camp.

The number of Jewish residents in Feldafing was increasing each day, as survivors entered from all over Europe. More than five thousand Jews were already in Feldafing, and since there was no alternative they ate from the nonkosher central camp kitchen. The Rebbe felt a compelling need to do something about the situation.

Two of the Rebbe's followers, Yechezkel Samet and Baruch

Ganz, accepted the task of organizing a kosher kitchen. After much effort they were able to obtain a large quantity of utensils from the main camp warehouse. After making them kosher in accordance with the Rebbe's instructions, they set up a full kitchen with separate sections for meat and dairy. Next they obtained a large supply of food from the camp storage facilities and some other places and began providing hot meals to anyone who requested.

The Rebbe made sure that the kosher kitchen sent food regularly to typhus patients in the camp hospital who desired it. He also set up a special organization called "Bikur Cholim" for that purpose.

A Father to Orphans

Next the Rebbe turned his attention to the dozens of young orphans living in the camp with no one to look out for them. The Rebbe felt it was his obligation to involve himself in their spiritual needs and to care for them as a surrogate father. In addition to providing for their needs, he worried over them like a biological parent.

Almost fifty years later, after the Rebbe's passing, his family was visited during shivah by a woman who had been in Feldafing. She told the family how as a young girl she had been so poor that she walked around the DP camp with no socks. Upon seeing her one day, the Rebbe took off his socks in the middle of the street and gave them to her, saying, "It is unbecoming for a Jewish girl to have to walk around this way."[1]

Lieutenant Meyer Birnbaum, the religious American army officer, related that an American official informed the Rebbe

---

1 Reported by Chaim Mendel Steiger.

that there was a group of Hungarian Jewish girls in the Foehrenwald DP camp who had completely forgotten their roots and were behaving inappropriately. Without hesitation, the Rebbe immediately departed for Foehrenwald in search of these girls. When he found them, he began to speak to them kindly and compassionately in Hungarian. After a long talk he convinced most of them to return with him to Feldafing.

Back in Feldafing, the Rebbe established a school for these girls, who had all come from strictly observant homes, and they returned to a religious way of life. Sometimes the girls would come to him and cry bitterly about their lives and the suffering they had experienced. The Rebbe would listen to them intently and gently offer words of healing and encouragement.[2]

Taking Care of "His" Children

On the Rebbe's initiative a second kosher kitchen was opened in Feldafing, this one especially for the children. The Rebbe oversaw its operation and made sure that it was always well supplied. When there was insufficient food in the camp, the Rebbe insisted that the children be fed first and the adults forgo their portion. Once he learned that the butcher was going to strike because of a work-related dispute. This would result in the young children going hungry. He hurriedly went to meet with the butcher and convinced him with gentle but firm words to return to work.[3]

Each morning the Rebbe went to ritually immerse himself in the stream that flowed next to the camp. As he passed the chil-

---

2 Birnbaum, p. 153–154.
3 Reported by Baruch Ganz.

dren's barracks, he threw candy in through the windows. He also prevailed upon Moshe Levi Hertz to learn *Maseches Beitzah* every day with the boys, about fifty in number. From Rosh Chodesh Elul until after Shabbos Bereishis, Moshe Levi also taught them *Musarei Rambam*, a *sefer* by Rabbi Shimon Sofer, son of the Kesav Sofer, which had been brought to the camp from Munich. The Rebbe also gathered together four teenage boys and established the first yeshivah in the DP camp. Rabbi Alexander (Sender) Dirnfeld was selected as their teacher.

"How Could I Have Done Differently?"

Today the Rebbe's actions seem unremarkable — indeed, a natural course of events. However, when one considers the spiritual and emotional condition of the survivors at that time — how they had just been rescued from hell on earth, how many of them had difficulty just thinking — then the awesome nature of the Rebbe's actions comes into much sharper focus. His success in returning Jewish children to the study of Torah was something only an extraordinary person could accomplish.

Years later, the Rebbe was asked what had motivated him to be so active and so determined immediately after his liberation. The Rebbe responded humbly, "I saw piles of corpses around me. How could I not bring them to a proper Jewish burial? All around me were sick people, people who had suffered terribly. How could I not care for them? Hundreds of orphans wandered aimlessly around the camps; surely someone had to gather them together and establish a home for them. How could I have stood by and done nothing?"

172 The Klausenberger Rebbe: The War Years

Lacking Nothing

After liberation the Rebbe did not have a penny to his name. He had not yet established a relationship with representatives of the Joint Distribution Committee, nor had he received any assistance from organizations and individuals outside the camps. Nonetheless, with great faith and confidence in the Almighty he opened the first yeshivah in the DP camps.

In his *sefer Shefa Chaim*, the Rebbe related the following story: A guest from America once came to the Feldafing DP camp for several days. He was present at one of the Rebbe's classes in halachah to the students of the yeshivah. "Do they lack anything?" the man asked.

The Rebbe answered, "I am teaching them to ask for nothing. Therefore they will have enough. When one acquires knowledge, what else does he need?"[4]

The Leader of Hungarian Survivors

A report issued shortly after liberation about the Jews in Feldafing stated, "The observant Jews living in Feldafing can be divided into three groups. The largest group by far are the Hungarian Jews, headed by a towering individual, the Klausenberger Rebbe. The second group are the Polish Jews, led by several rabbis and young community leaders from Agudas Yisrael. The third group are Lithuanian Jews, headed by a number of Talmudic scholars from Kovna. They are concerned with the reestablishment of religious life not only in the camp in which they live but in other locations, as well.

---

4 *Shefa Chaim*, vol. 2, p. 146.

"The Klausenberger Rebbe, a dynamic personality, has quickly spread his influence over the masses of Jews in all the DP camps under American control. He is the only Hungarian chassidic leader who has survived the war who is now on German soil. It is therefore no wonder that Hungarian survivors of all types are drawn to him for both encouragement and guidance. Several other important Hungarian rabbis, including Rabbi Yehudah Gottleib of Miskolc, Rabbi Yoel Tzvi Rota of Tisa-Salki, and Rabbi Yechezkel Rutner of Shamkot, are also presently in Feldafing. But the Klausenberger Rebbe stands out among them all."[5]

News of the Rebbe's survival quickly spread among the survivors and the Jewish world at large. The Jerusalem newspaper *Kol Yisrael* reported in its issue of 17 Tammuz, 1945, under the headline "Greetings from the Klausenberger Rebbe," "Our teacher [Rav Yosef Tzvi Dushinsky] received the news that the great Rabbi Yekusiel Yehudah Halberstam, the Klausenberger Rebbe, is alive in Germany." The city of Klausenberg was no longer merely a European city; it now represented a large group of survivors, men, women, and children, who were devoted followers of the Rebbe.

The "Kosher Home"

One survivor, Mordechai Taub, recalled, "When I was liberated from the Germans I was a young boy in the Garmish concentration camp. There were no religious Jews anywhere nearby, but I heard that in Feldafing there was a yeshivah with a

---

5 Yosef Friedenson in *Dos Yiddishe Vort* 253 (New York: Nissan/Iyar 1985), p. 37.

dormitory for religious boys. The survivors referred to it as the 'kosher home.' I did not know exactly who was in charge of it, but when I got there, along with my brother and a few friends, we found before us a merciful father, whom we so desperately needed. He was the Klausenberger Rebbe."

Matisyahu Prizel related the following: "The Rebbe circulated among the forlorn children who had been gathered together from many different concentration camps. He fed them with love and real concern and taught them to recite the Shema.

"I was too old to associate with the group of children, but emotionally I was drawn to them because I felt like I had been born anew. I was very close to the Rebbe and he brought me closer to him.

"Sometimes the Rebbe taught the children *chumash*, sprinkling his lesson with parables and heartwarming stories. Other times he would say things that frightened us, such as 'You should know, my beloved children, that your holy parents are spreading their wings over you. Their blessed souls are surely hovering over you, longing to absorb every sacred word that comes out of your mouths.' "

Every morning, the Rebbe would come into the children's barracks. The youngsters, deeply scarred by the horrors of the Holocaust, had not yet recovered from the suffering which they had endured. They needed a great deal of support and encouragement. The Rebbe always came immediately after davening, asking each child what he needed, talking to him on his own level. The children told him everything — where they came from, what their background was, who their parents were, and how they had survived.

"How were you saved?" the Rebbe asked each child, seeking to arouse feelings of faith in God and to train the child to look to the Almighty for his needs.

All the children called the Rebbe by the same name: "Tatte!" They were so attached to him that once when American supervisors came to transfer a group of children to another DP camp, they hid all over the camp so that they would not be forced to leave the Rebbe.[6]

One day, several generals from the Allied armies came to see the camp. A group of communists in the camp organized a demonstration and confronted the generals with all sorts of demands, holding a red flag. The Rebbe's response to this was to organize his own demonstration. Carrying a flag emblazoned with the words "*Mi laShem eilai* — He who is to God come to me," the Rebbe attracted the attention of the religious survivors and was soon surrounded by a number of people, including all the children in the camp. Holding a Torah scroll in his arms, he danced enthusiastically with the children.[7]

"Our Eyes Are Fixed on the Land of Israel"

Despite the fact that the Rebbe was still dressed in the garments he had been given immediately after liberation, with nothing to distinguish him from any other survivor, he drew people toward him like a magnet. (Only after leaving Feldafing was he given a rabbinic hat.) He quietly reestablished the prewar practices of a chassidic Rebbe, reading petitions, giving advice, and conferring blessings on anyone who came to him.

---

6 Reported by Matisyahu Prizel.
7 See note above.

One of the Rebbe's self-appointed tasks was guiding the survivors to making the right decisions about their futures. Many survivors wanted to return to their prewar homes in Hungary, Romania, and Czechoslovakia, either not realizing the extent of the destruction or hoping to find surviving family members. But the Rebbe tried to convince them that it was best for the time being to remain in the DP camp. "We have nothing more to do in those blood-soaked lands," he said.

Although many of the survivors viewed emigration to America as the ticket to the future, the Rebbe was quick to remind them that the Land of Israel is the Jewish people's true home. One day the Rebbe spoke to a Russian general, a Jew by birth, who came to Feldafing to perform *chalitzah* with his sister-in-law. The two spoke for several hours about the plight of the survivors in Germany, and the general made several suggestions for their future. Among his suggestions was to establish settlements for Jews in Ethiopia, where they would be able to rebuild their lives anew with the economic assistance of the United States and its allies. The Rebbe's immediate response was, "We do not want to live among the gentiles! Our eyes are fixed on Eretz Yisrael."[8]

The Rebbe had long dreamed of moving to the Land of Israel. At one time during the Holocaust, when it seemed that all hope was lost, the Rebbe vowed, "If Hashem will be with me and I leave this hell alive, then I will be careful all my life not to take pleasure from any human being; I will leave the Diaspora and live in Eretz Yisrael; and I will make every effort to instill love and unity among the Jewish people."[9]

---

8 Based on a written account approved by the Rebbe.
9 See note above.

Healing All Souls

Many of the survivors were very confused about their futures. Antireligious propaganda filled the camp, telling them that the only thing that would save the Jewish people from all its troubles was assimilation. The Rebbe, who persisted in advocating the obligation to rebuild Jewish life and return it to its former glory, was a constant thorn in the sides of the antireligious agents. "Your approach will bring another Hitler on us!" they would yell at him in the streets of Feldafing.[10] But the Rebbe paid no heed to his opposition and continued to openly express his views — that the oppressed Jew would only be rescued from his oppressors when he held onto the anchor of Torah and mitzvos.

Besides serving as a source of personal advice and material needs for survivors, the Rebbe healed enormous emotional wounds. One survivor, Shalom Eliyahu Pelberbaum, recalled, "I was extremely weak after a bout of typhus, nearly at death's door. I was confined to bed and couldn't even move on my own. But when I was brought to the *beis midrash* on Friday night and heard the Rebbe's prayers, I came alive. He poured his heart out, emotionally repeating the words over and over again: '*Kol Hashem b'koach* — The voice of God is in power! *Kol Hashem behadar* — The voice of God is in majesty!' Every word renewed in me a desire to live.

"One day I heard that the Rebbe had somehow obtained for himself a pair of Rabbeinu Tam tefillin. I desperately wanted to put them on and went to his room to ask for permission to use the tefillin. When I came in, the Rebbe was deeply absorbed in

10 Reported by Yehoshua Veitzenblum.

studying a *Talmud Yerushalmi* and did not notice me. I sat down and waited. Two and a half hours went by, and the Rebbe was so immersed in his learning that he did not realize that I was there. When he finished learning he lifted his eyes, surprised to see me, and asked what I needed. I asked him to lend me his Rabbeinu Tam tefillin. He didn't want me to remove them from his room but agreed wholeheartedly that I come to his room every day and put them on there."

Chapter 14

A New Year Begins

In Defense of His People

As the high holidays approached, the Rebbe spent
much time speaking publicly. His message was both
comforting and inspiring. Many survivors returned
to Torah observance during that period.[1] In the words of one
commentator, "As hard as it is to understand God's actions during a time of *hester panim*, it is all the more difficult to understand how the Jewish people were able to remain strong in their
faith."[2]

The Rebbe's speeches never failed to move his audience. He
spoke directly to the Almighty, as if to rebuke Him, recalling the
millions of human sacrifices and the suffering and persecutions
inflicted on millions more. Yet with all this, "We did not forget
You and did not violate Your covenant." The Rebbe never mentioned a word about his own enormous personal tragedy; he
spoke only of the tragedy of the Jewish people.

The Rebbe noted that the Nazis murdered not only people

1 Reported by Yosef Friedenson in *Dos Yiddishe Vort* 327 (Tishrei 1996), p. 22.
2 See *Dos Yiddishe Vort* 253, p. 30.

who identified themselves as Jews but also Jews who had long since converted to Christianity. "When Mashiach will come and we will merit the true redemption," he said, "a prosecuting angel will surely tell the Almighty that He should only redeem those who remained strong when they were in exile. But Hashem will respond, 'During the days of persecution they were all considered Jews, whether or not they served Me. Now that the redemption has come, should they not be considered Jews?' "

The Rebbe's listeners, who had been so dulled to pain that they had lost the ability to cry, now cried along with him. The Rebbe spoke of the greatness of the Jewish people and defended them, imploring the Almighty to bring the final redemption speedily. Continuing his speech, the Rebbe challenged the survivors not to forget their origins and thus lose the merits which they had accumulated through their suffering.

The Rebbe was careful not to give his followers false hopes. Once, during a *tisch*, his brother-in-law, Rabbi Yechiel Yehudah Isaacson, commented that surely the suffering during the Holocaust had been the birth pangs of Mashiach and Mashiach would soon arrive. The Rebbe responded immediately, "From where do you know this? Who is privy to the secrets of Hashem? During World War I, a period of great suffering, someone said to my father, 'Rebbe, the time has come for the Jewish people to be redeemed from exile.' My father sighed and said, 'I am very much afraid that more suffering will come upon us before Mashiach comes.' He added, 'I am prepared to pay a full *rendel* for every peek into the heavens that they will allow me.' "

The Rebbe continued, "I am prepared to pay a whole trunk full of money for just one peek. But what can I do — our eyes have been closed. The future has been hidden from us and no one knows when Mashiach will come."[3]

In the Shul and in the Street

The Rebbe's speeches had a tremendous impact. Hundreds of listeners, whether in shul or at his Shabbos *tisch*, were aroused and inspired to return to Torah observance. After every speech, repentant souls crowded around him.

Avraham Getzel Schiff reported, "When I came to Germany from Russia in 1946 people told me wondrous things about the Rebbe's speeches in the main streets of Feldafing and Munich, much like the prophet Yirmiyahu who stood in the streets of Jerusalem urging the people of his day to return to God. But one difference between the Rebbe and Yirmiyahu was that the generation of Yirmiyahu did not listen to him and threw him into a pit, saying, 'This man is a son of death.' The Holocaust survivors in Germany, however, drank in the words of the Klausenberger Rebbe thirstily. Many, in the hundreds and thousands, repented as a result of his influence."

"Your Children Shall Return to Their Borders"

One of the most powerful of the Rebbe's speeches was the one he gave to the huge crowd which had gathered to daven with him on the second day of Rosh HaShanah. The speech was based on a lecture of the Noda BeYehudah, Rabbi Yechezkel Landau of Prague (*Drushei HaTzelach* 18). It should be noted, however, that the Rebbe had no access to the Noda BeYehudah's

---

3 Reported by Rabbi Y. A. Zalmanovitz.

sefer at the time and gave the discourse entirely from memory.

The Rebbe began with a verse from the haftarah: "So said God: A voice was heard on high — wailing, bitter weeping — Rachel weeps for her children, she refuses to be consoled for her children, for they are gone" (*Yirmiyahu* 31:14). "Why does the prophet repeat the words 'her children'?" asked the Rebbe. "Wouldn't it have been sufficient to say, 'She refuses to be consoled for they are gone'?

"The prophet is telling us," the Rebbe explained, "that there are two types of suffering that the Divine Presence suffers when the Jewish people are in exile. [In Kabbalah, "Rachel" refers to the Divine Presence.] The first, referred to in the phrase 'Rachel weeps for her children,' is suffering for the physical persecution that has befallen the Jews. Whenever the Jewish people are being persecuted, the Divine Presence feels pain, too. The second suffering is the pain which the Divine Presence feels for the Jews who, as a result of their persecution, stray from the Torah and forget that they are descendants of a holy people. This is the suffering 'for her children, for they are gone'; they have ceased to be the children of Hashem.

"Besides the great embarrassment of being considered servants of Hashem, rather than His children, this demotion brings with it great peril and the danger of complete destruction. Our Sages (in *Sanhedrin* 111a) disagreed over the interpretation of the verse 'And I shall take you, one from a city and two from a family [and I will bring you to Tzion]' (*Yirmiyahu* 3:14). Rabbi Shimon ben Lakish was of the opinion that the verse was to be understood literally — when the Jewish people are sent to exile, only one from a city and two from a family will remain. Rabbi

Yochanan, however, explained that one individual will save an entire city and one from a family will save the entire family.

"The Noda BeYehudah explained: If the Jewish people remain on the level of sons, then each one will feel a close family connection to one another and will feel the sorrow of another, and then it will be possible for each to save his friends and relatives. But if the Jews are on the level of slaves, who are unrelated and do not care about one another, then the verse must be fulfilled in its literal sense, and only one from the city and two from a family will survive.

"Due to our many sins," the Rebbe cried out, "this terrible prophecy has come to fruition. 'Rachel weeps for her children' — for those who have been murdered *al kiddush haShem*. Besides this, the Divine Presence refuses to be comforted 'for her children, for they are gone' — the Jews who have survived have forgotten their origins and have lost the appellation of children. Look and see what has happened to us: Only one from a city and two from a family have survived the crematoria!"

The Rebbe then explained the next verse in the haftarah: "So says God: Restrain your voice from weeping and your eyes from tears; for there is a reward for your accomplishment, says God, and they shall return from the enemy's land. There is hope for you ultimately, says God, and your children shall return to their border" (*Yirmiyahu* 31:15–16).

"Here, too, the verses seem to repeat themselves. First it says, 'And they shall return from the enemy's land,' and then it says, 'And your children shall return to their border.' It is clear that these verses parallel the two types of suffering referred to in the earlier verse. Rachel's weeping for her children's suffering is answered with the promise that 'they shall return from the enemy's land.' In response to her unwillingness to be comforted for her children no longer being God's children, Hashem promises, 'Your children shall return to their border' — they will regain their former position of beloved children of Hashem!

"The process of the Jewish people's return to Hashem," continued the Rebbe, "will occur in phases. First, they shall return from the enemy's land — even in exile, the Jews will begin to repent, before they are on the level of children of Hashem. Afterwards, 'Your children shall return to their border' — they will repent out of love and reclaim their title as Hashem's children. Our Sages teach us that if the Jewish people are not worthy of redemption at the end of days, the Almighty will issue harsh decrees against them — decrees which we have already suffered at the hands of Hitler, *yemach shemo* — and this will bring them back. Thus the Almighty promises, 'Your children shall return to their borders' — they will be considered children once again.

"Holy Jews!" the Rebbe cried out with great emotion, "listen to the pained voice of the Divine Presence which refuses to be comforted for its children who are gone — for the many survivors who are no longer children of Hashem and who are barely recognizable as Jews. My brothers, let us return to our Father in Heaven! Let us become once again Jews worthy of being called 'children of God'! Let us take upon ourselves the yoke of His kingdom! Only then will Hashem's promise be fulfilled through us: 'And your children shall return to their border.' "[4]

---

4 Reported by David Greenzweig.

Vidui of the Survivors

On *erev Yom Kippur*, the Rebbe was very weak. Reb Moshe Levi Hertz, who taught the boys in the DP camp, relates: "When I went to ask the Rebbe to bless the boys in my care, he was so weak that he said he would bless them only after Yom Kippur began. Nevertheless, as soon as night fell, he somehow marshaled his strength and went to the *beis midrash* to lead the prayers. His activity that night was simply beyond belief."

After *Kol Nidrei*, the Rebbe went to stand next to the open ark and began to speak, directing his words toward Heaven. Crying bitterly, the Rebbe spoke not from the *machzor* in his hands but straight from his heart. In a wholly unorthodox manner he called out the words of *Vidui*: "*Ashamnu, bagadnu* (we have sinned, we have rebelled)...." Each word was inflected not as a statement but as a question: "Did we sin? Did we rebel?"

Almost accusatorily, the Rebbe asked, "Did we really sin? Did we really rebel? Did we, *chas veshalom*, rebel against You and fail to remain faithful? *Gazalnu* — did we steal? From whom did we steal in Auschwitz and Muldorf? Was there anybody to steal from?"

Suddenly, the Rebbe paused for a moment. "Yes, I am a thief! I admit it. One day when I returned from the slave labor I collapsed onto my bunk in the barracks to rest, and my shriveled skin got caught between two boards. When I tried to free myself with what little strength I had left, my skin tore from my bones. Blood streamed out, and I moaned softly. But my moan was loud enough to wake a fellow prisoner sleeping next to me. Yes, I stole. I stole sleep from an exhausted person. This is the only theft I committed and I admit it before the Master of the Universe. I have sinned!"

Then the Rebbe continued reciting the words of the *machzor*: "*Dibarnu dofi* — we spoke slander? We never even had enough strength for idle conversation. If by chance we had any remaining strength, we saved it so that we would be able to answer the questions of our vicious oppressors! *He'evinu* — we caused perversion? *Hirshanu* — we caused wickedness? Who? Us? *Latznu* — we scorned? Who could do such a thing there? *Maradnu* — we rebelled? Against whom? We rebelled against the Almighty? Didn't we suffer every beating quietly with the knowledge that 'You are righteous in everything that comes upon us'?! We rebelled against our oppressors? Could we have rebelled against them even if we had tried?"

Word by word, the Rebbe dismissed each and every alleged sin of the survivors. "We did not commit evil acts. We did not sin willfully! This *vidui* was not written for us," he concluded, closing his *machzor*. His congregation stood in shock.

After a second pause, the Rebbe raised his voice again. "But we are guilty of sins that are not written in the *machzor*. We sinned in our faith and trust in our Creator. Did we not doubt Hashem out of despair and hopelessness in the camps? When we recited Shema at night, we hoped that it would be our last *HaMapil*, that the end of our suffering would come. How many times did we pray, 'Master of the Universe, I have no more strength. Take my soul so I will not have to recite *Modeh Ani* anymore'? And when the sun rose and we were obligated to thank Hashem for 'returning my soul with great mercy,' we were consumed with anger and rage. When we removed the corpses from the barracks, weren't we jealous of those lucky people who had died?

"This is how we have sinned. We sinned with a lack of faith and trust. We must beat our chests and admit our sins. We must ask the Almighty to restore our faith and trust in Him. 'Trust in God forever.' 'Trust in Him at all times, nation! Pour your hearts out before Him.' "[5]

Appearing before Dignitaries

The following day, in the middle of Yom Kippur, the Feldafing camp residents were visited by the supreme Allied commander General Dwight D. Eisenhower, who later became president of the United States. The camp residents all gathered to greet him at the entrance to the camp. The Rebbe came to welcome the general with a gift of a braided challah and salt, the customary gift for a gentile ruler, in one hand and a Torah scroll in the other.

In honor of General Eisenhower's visit, a royal welcoming ceremony had been organized. The majority of the survivors wanted the Rebbe to be the main speaker, feeling that he could best express the survivors' feelings and needs. However, the leadership of the irreligious factions stridently objected to this, announcing that they would not allow the Rebbe to speak unless he agreed not to make any mention of God or Judaism in his speech. The Rebbe also could only speak for a few short moments and others would address the gathering, as well.

The Rebbe paid no heed to these instructions. As he went up to the speaker's platform, someone handed him a tallis,

---

5 Birnbaum, p. 163–166.

which the Rebbe slipped under his arm. When he reached the platform, he unfurled the tallis in the air, recited the blessing *LeHisateif BeTzitzis*, and wrapped the tallis around himself in full view of the entire crowd.

The Rebbe's actions made an enormous emotional impact on the crowd. Seeing the Rebbe adorned in a tallis reminded all the survivors of their beloved parents and other loved ones who had been murdered in the sanctification of God's name. No one dared to utter a sound.

As total silence reigned, the Rebbe began to speak. In a thundering voice, he spoke of the destruction and the suffering, the lot of the Jewish people and their role in the world as the Chosen People, the nation of Hashem.

Although he began his speech by blessing General Eisenhower, the honored guest, who had been chosen by heaven to perform the great kindness of liberating an innocent people taken to slaughter, his words were directed primarily to the survivors, challenging them never to forget their heritage. Next he demanded of the "enlightened" and "cultured" countries of the world never to forget what the Nazis had done to the Jewish people. He spoke with an extraordinary strength, and his emotions heightened moment by moment. The crowd of some eight thousand survivors was swept along with him. Tears streamed down every face; grown men wept like babies.

When the Rebbe finished speaking, he instructed the chazzan, Aharon Miller, to recite *Keil Malei Rachamim* for the merit of the holy martyrs. As the words were recited, the crowd wept bitterly. The welcoming ceremony had become an extraordinary sanctification of God's name.

The atmosphere of the crowd changed completely. The Rebbe's antagonists from the left "forgave" him for mentioning God, and the speakers who were supposed to follow him no longer wished to speak. Lieutenant Meyer Birnbaum translated every word of the Rebbe's speech for General Eisenhower, who was visibly affected by the speech and promised to do everything in his power to help the survivors.

A special relationship of mutual respect developed between the Rebbe and General Eisenhower — a relationship which lasted many years and was utilized several times for the benefit of the religious community.

At the conclusion of the ceremony, the general asked the Rebbe, "In what way can I help you now?" The Rebbe answered through the translator that he had but one request. Could the General arrange for the Rebbe and the rest of the survivors to have a set of the four species for the holiday of Sukkos?

Upon hearing this request, General Eisenhower was deeply moved. He realized that the survivor standing before him was a man of God. There was no other way to explain why a survivor in a DP camp, when asked personally by the supreme Allied commander for anything that he wished, would ask only for a set of the four species.

A special military plane was sent to Italy on General Eisenhower's command to pick up *lulavim* and *esrogim*, which were brought back to the Feldafing DP camp for the Rebbe and his followers.[6]

---

6 Reported by Yehoshua Veitzenblum.

Chapter 15

A New Court for the Rebbe

Moving to Foehrenwald

Feldafing could no longer handle the huge number of survivors who filled it, many of whom had come because of its large community of Orthodox Jews. The authorities of the American sector therefore had to arrange for the opening of another large DP camp. They chose a former military base in Foehrenwald, also located in the Munich area, which was several times larger than the Feldafing camp and would serve well as a relatively comfortable temporary home for the survivors. The camp administrators suggested to the Rebbe that he transfer to Foehrenwald.

The Rebbe planned to take under his wings hundreds of surviving youth and establish educational institutions for them. He received an assurance from the camp administrators that a complete section of apartments and small villas, previously occupied by the *Wehrmacht*, would be put at his disposal in Foehrenwald, and it would be possible to develop a broader network of religious institutions and services. The Rebbe therefore decided to leave Feldafing, together with all the children in the camp, and transfer to Foehrenwald.

Immediately after Yom Kippur, the Rebbe established his living quarters in Foehrenwald. The DP camp quickly became an important Torah center, the center of the activities of the She'eiris HaPleitah in the DP camps throughout Europe.

She'eiris HaPleitah

Although the survivors had been liberated from the concentration camps by the Allied forces, they were still not free to go where they pleased. The DP camps in Germany, France, and Italy were both their homes and their prisons. It was impossible to return to their prewar homes — the houses had been destroyed and anti-Semitism was rampant throughout Europe. Israel was out of the reach because of the cruel limits on immigration imposed by the British, then in control of the land. The rest of the world, including the United States, the "*malchus shel chesed*," closed their doors, albeit for only a time, to the survivors.

The survivors were concentrated mainly in the American sector of Germany, though some were in the British sector, and a few were in the French sector and in the western sections of Berlin. Their lives were officially organized by central organizations which operated mainly in Munich, Bergen-Belsen, and Berlin. These organizations were established specifically to take care of all the needs and the problems of the survivors. However, these organizations were all controlled by irreligious and Zionist factions.

Immediately after his liberation, the Rebbe decided to establish a network of communal organizations for religious Jews so that they would no longer be dependent on the irreligious parties, which were far from supporting or understanding the needs of the religious community. This network, which included both Torah institutions and general social and welfare institutions, was called "She'eiris HaPleitah."

A Declaration on the Survivors' Behalf

A few days before leaving Feldafing, during the Ten Days of Repentance, the Rebbe wrote the following moving declaration to the Jews in free countries, pleading them to fulfill their duty and help the destitute survivors. His fiery words gave voice to the cries of thousands of survivors.

To our Jewish brethren:

As a result of our sins, we, the Jews of Europe, have suffered years of persecution, in which the evil oppressors, may their names be obliterated, rose against us to wipe out, kill, and destroy, God forbid, all the Jews. During all those years, no one rose to share our suffering or to assist us. The "one from a city and two from a family" who remain survived only through the promise of our holy Torah, "I will not cast them away, nor will I abhor them" (Vayikra 26:44), and by the covenant that the Jewish people will not be destroyed (Bava Basra 115b). Yet though we have been freed from slavery, we have not yet gained freedom.

Klal Yisrael has been exiled time and again, each Jew going from place to place in search of his lost ones – father, mother, wife, children, and relatives – lost and confused in the land of his enemy, the murderers of his family. Burning tears stream down our faces seeing our enemies already content and at peace. The prison gates have already been opened for them and they are returning to their homes and families, living comfortably and serenely, while we are homeless, impoverished, and mourning for our loved ones.

All the doors have been shut, locked before us. Even the gates to our holy land, the land of our dreams, are closed to us. We are kept in camps in poverty and shame. Twenty people sleep on bunk beds in very small rooms, one on top of the other, without clothing and without shoes. Imagine for yourselves this bizarre scene. In our camp of some five thousand Jews from all over Europe, many are still wearing the brown shirts of the Hitler Youth, may their names be obliterated. They have not been able to remove their degrading prison uniforms yet.

With regard to food, although it is four months since our liberation and we have established — under very difficult circumstances — a kosher kitchen, we are still unable to feed all those seeking kosher food because our supply of food is simply insufficient. Thus, many of our fellow Jews are forced to continue eating nonkosher food, which is also in limited supply. Even though we have received a few small shipments of two or three kilograms from America, they hardly made a difference. It is true that organizations and offices have been opened under a variety of names, but they have not yet accomplished anything. I can honestly say that to date absolutely nothing of value has reached the camps.

Isn't it your responsibility to care for the remnants of your European brethren, particularly the thousands who are sick with tuberculosis and typhus? Even though the military commander of our camp, Lieutenant Smith, is trying hard to improve our situation, his hands are also tied, and he too does not have the resources available to supply everything we need.

On top of all this, our hearts ache because literally a hundred men grab onto a single tallis which one person received from a relative. Men wait for hours to use a pair of tefillin so as to recite the first paragraph of the Shema, and holy Jews who survived among the millions who went to their deaths in the crematoria crowd together and look from afar at a page from a siddur. They waste innumerable hours with no Torah books because none of these items can be found in this entire country. Even during these holy days no one has been aroused to supply our needs – not even to provide us with kosher Torah scrolls, tefillin, mezuzos, tzitzis, siddurim, machzorim, chumashim, mishnayos, and the like.

I have been silent until now because I thought that the feelings of mercy would be aroused in my fellow Jews, compassionate people, people involved in good deeds. However, my pain does not allow me to remain silent any longer. I call out, again and again, to the heads of every committee and organization – Where are you?

Jewish nation! Have you examined your deeds before your Creator? Have you fulfilled your obligations to your brothers who are withering away from agony, living in the valley of tears, fearful of what the next day will bring? In the morning, the few thousand souls who survived ask when night will come, and in the night, they ask when the morning will arrive – and this after years of persecution at the hand of the evil oppressors, may their names be obliterated.

On behalf of all the holy martyrs who were murdered and burned alive in the sanctification of the name Yisrael, we scream: Please save us! Don't wait any longer! Volunteer quickly! Come to the aid of Hashem for the sake of these mighty ones!

Please take care that your assistance really reaches those who are needy and that no one interferes along the way.

Writing with a broken heart, longing for the Almighty's salvation, and blessing the Jewish people with a g'mar chasimah tovah,

Rabbi Yekusiel Yehudah Halberstam
Av Beis Din of Klausenberg

"Open for Me the Gates of Righteousness"

The Rebbe's greatest hour came in Foehrenwald. The *Hallel* he recited one Rosh Chodesh in this camp epitomized his longings for his Creator and his hopes for the future. As he recited each verse, he added his own words in Yiddish, like a small child speaking to his father. " 'God chastened me exceedingly, but He did not let me die,' " he cried out. "Oh, how You have chastened me, Master of the Universe, simply by not letting me die in the sanctification of Your holy name like Your other pure and holy children. "Now that You have given me life, I beseech You, 'Open for me the gates of righteousness; I will enter them and praise God.' Please grant me the ability to praise Your holy name and to spread the belief in Your oneness in this world![1]

"I know I am unworthy for this task. They have responded to me from Heaven: 'This gate through which you request to pass is the gate to God; only the righteous shall enter through it.' But I will continue to plead with You, Master of the Universe, until the gates are opened for me. I will not be silent until I am granted entry. Open for me the gate of righteousness; I will enter through them and praise God!"[2]

---

1 Reported by Yehoshua Veitzenblum.
2 Reported by Moshe Weiss.

The gates of righteousness were indeed opened for the Rebbe, and he passed through them to glorify the Almighty's name in the world. He did not sanctify God's name by sacrificing his life; instead, he did it by remaining alive and dedicating himself to the resurgence of Jewish life.

An article in a religious newspaper reported: "Just enter the gates of Foehrenwald and you will immediately feel as if you are in a Galician, Polish, or Hungarian village saturated with Jewish life.... Between the barracks walks the Klausenberger Rebbe, the person responsible for making the Foehrenwald camp into the center of religious Jewish life for all the DP camps. Everyone who comes to Foehrenwald feels uplifted by the holiness that permeates the camp."[3]

Taking Action for the Survivors' Material Needs

Despite the fact that the Rebbe was a penniless survivor himself, he was completely dedicated to the needs of the survivors around him, even to his own detriment. He worked tirelessly to make sure that the survivors had food and other material necessities. It wasn't long before his petition to General Eisenhower about the plight of the survivors in Feldafing bore fruit. Once, food and clothing packages arrived from the United States, but the head of the UNRWA refused to release them because they claimed that the necessary paperwork was missing. General Eisenhower, remembering the Rebbe from their meeting on Yom Kippur, immediately ordered that the packages be distributed.[4]

---

3 Quoted from *"Ir V'Eim BeYisrael"* (A leading city in Jewry), *Kol Yisrael BaGolah* (23 Av 1946).

4 Discovered by an investigation conducted under the Rebbe's direction.

On Rosh Chodesh Cheshvan, only a few weeks after the Rebbe's relocation to Foehrenwald, a large group of young survivors arrived in the camp. The group was composed of tens of young men and women from Galician chassidic families, including several descendants of the Divrei Chaim, who had been settled in temporary DP camps in the Russian sector. Longing for a religious environment, they had decided to cross over into the American sector when they had heard about the Klausenberger Rebbe. After a long and a difficult journey, they reached Foehrenwald and the Rebbe's open arms.

Knowing that there was no other available housing, the Rebbe immediately had his followers take over a row of empty houses in the camp, even though the camp authorities had refused to give them to religious survivors. "If anyone comes to interfere or arrest you," the Rebbe instructed, "tell them that you are acting under my orders and that I take full responsibility."

Although this action caused an uproar, the result was that an entire street in the camp, known as New York Street, became a strictly religious neighborhood.[5]

A Spiritual Savior

The Rebbe's motto was "Renew our days as of old." The Jewish people had to return to the complete Jewish life of their forefathers, and no compromises or deviations could be tolerated. The Rebbe clung to this vision alone. Those around him, even great and well-meaning people, did not believe that after all that had occurred it was possible to dream of rebuilding Jewish life as it had been before the Holocaust. The Rebbe not only believed

---

5 Reported by Yehoshua Veitzenblum.

that it was possible, but he also felt it his personal responsibility to turn that vision into a reality.

One of the Rebbe's followers, Yosef Yitzchak Cohen, reported at the time:

"If the physical condition of the concentration camp survivors during the first several months after liberation was tragic, their spiritual and religious condition was even more desperate. Anyone who dared to speak of religious feelings was regarded as crazy, and someone who dreamed of the establishment of a yeshivah and of a vibrant religious life was hallucinating. It was simply impossible to even think of such things. A giant was required; one with the spirit, energy and determination to rise above the other survivors, those frail skeletons, and reinvigorate them with a grand vision; a leader who would lead them day and night with total selflessness and devotion until his ideas penetrated into the depths of their hearts and they returned to their source, the Torah, which would heal them.

"This exalted leader appeared in the person of the illustrious Klausenberger Rebbe, who recognized the challenge of the time and took upon himself the great and holy task of rescuing his fellow survivors from spiritual and religious destruction. As one who experienced the Holocaust himself, he found the key to the people's hearts.... He focused especially on the young people, whose souls had been through the fiery furnace and could thus accept the Torah through affliction.

"Old in suffering but young in years, these children had been snatched from their loving parents and longed for a warm home, a kind word, and a loving environment. The Klausenberger Rebbe came to them with fatherly compassion and warm words sprinkled with moral lessons...and found the key to their souls. He was a father to them in both the physical and spiritual senses. He succeeded in accomplishing his holy goals because of his unlimited and immeasurable dedication and selflessness."[6]

Thousands of people from the DP camps throughout Germany flocked to the Rebbe's court in Foehrenwald. Some came for a Shabbos and some for a *yom tov*, but all for the same reason — to be inspired by the Rebbe. For some just a single opportunity to hear the Rebbe daven was enough to motivate them to return to their roots. One such survivor recalled, "From behind, I saw the Rebbe praying, stretching his hands to the heavens and pleading, 'Behold our affliction.' At that moment, he won me over forever."[7]

Another survivor related, "When I heard the Rebbe cry his heart out to his Creator and beg Him, 'Master of the Universe, stop doing harm to the Jewish people — may they know no more trials and tribulations! Please do good, grant them only good!' I could not contain myself. I, too, began to pray."[8]

Making Do with the Barest Minimum

Except for Shabbos, the Rebbe never changed his clothes. He would make his rounds wearing torn *Wehrmacht* boots, firmly refusing to allow his followers to order new boots for him. "When they order new boots for all the survivors, you can order new ones for me," he told them.

Eventually, Moshe Eliezer Einhorn ordered new boots for

---

6 *Kol Yisrael BaGolah* 10 (8 Av 1947), p. 2.
7 Reported by Yehoshua Veitzenblum.
8 Reported by Moshe Weiss.

the Rebbe from a shoemaker in Munich. When they were ready, he entered the Rebbe's room in the early hours of the morning, when the Rebbe was finally asleep, removed the Rebbe's old boots from their place, and replaced them with new ones. When the Rebbe awakened he was extremely resentful about the abduction of his old shoes, but, having no choice, he was forced to put on the new ones.[9]

The Rebbe's sleep usually consisted of a short nap of two or three hours at the most, and sometimes much less. Yet he never appeared tired or lethargic. He once explained his secret. "It is a tradition from my grandfather, the Divrei Chaim, who would say that he slept quickly because someone blessed with a sharp mind is able to grasp in minutes concepts which take others hours to understand."[10]

When it came to eating, the Rebbe also made do with very little. When his followers would ask him when he would eat, he always had a ready answer: "Afterwards...later."

Once the Rebbe was driven from Foehrenwald to the slaughterhouse he had set up in Munich to observe its operations. After finishing his inspection of the slaughterhouse, he went to the office of the Central Committee for Liberated Jews in Munich to take care of several matters. By the time he had finished, it was time to daven minchah.

When he concluded Shemoneh Esrei, it had already gotten very late, so he quickly returned to the car for the trip back to Foehrenwald. His driver begged him to eat something, since he had not eaten all day.

---

9 Reported by Moshe Eliezer Einhorn.
10 Reported by Rabbi A. M. Jacobowitz.

"Soon," the Rebbe answered. "I first need to recite *Aleinu*."

When the Rebbe reached the words "to establish the universe with the Almighty's sovereignty," he was overcome with emotion and repeated the words over and over again. By the time he finished reciting *Aleinu*, they had already reached Foehrenwald.[11]

A Friday Night Tisch

On Friday nights the Rebbe conducted a *tisch* in his *beis midrash* in the presence of hundreds of students, chassidim, and other Jews from all over the camp. The following moving paragraphs are the impressions of Aryeh Avivi, a resident of Foehrenwald, recorded after attending one of these *tisches*:

"The hour was late. Chassidim as well as *misnagdim* began to gather for the Rebbe's *tisch*, and in a few short moments the *beis midrash* was filled to capacity. The chassidim piled on each other's shoulders, hung from the doors and windows, and climbed on benches and tables.

"The Rebbe entered with his closest followers and somehow a path opened for him to reach his table. He began to sing *Shalom Aleichem*. At first the words flowed softly, slowly. Then the pace intensified and his voice grew louder. The room was silent. It was as though the entire universe, heaven and earth, had stopped to listen to the prayers of this tzaddik. As his voice grew louder and louder, his fervor reminded me of the recitation of *U'Nesaneh Tokef* on Rosh HaShanah or the cry of '*Hashem Hu HaElokim*' during the final moments of Yom Kippur.

"As the Rebbe sang, '*Bo'achem leshalom*, may your coming

---

11 Reported by Yehoshua Veitzenblum.

be for peace, *malachei hashalom*, O angels of peace,' the words, uttered by his mouth, were expressed by his entire body. Although his face grew paler, his voice grew stronger and the pace of his movements grew faster. It was the first time in my life that I, a *misnaged*, had been so close to a chassidic Rebbe, let alone to the Klausenberger Rebbe, father of the orphans. As I absorbed his song-prayer, a new spirit filled me.

"I was not the only one so affected. Every person present, young and old alike, stood fixed in his place, mesmerized, forgetting entirely about the world around them. Just seeing the Rebbe and hearing his voice was enough to lift the weight of their agony and bring joy to their broken hearts. More than one shriveled heart returned to life through the Rebbe's prayers and songs, cries and groans, melodies and words of Torah.

"By the time the washing cup was brought before the Rebbe so he could wash his hands for the meal, the sun had already begun to rise over the despicable German skies. This was our dawn, too, a sign of our redemption, liberation, and upcoming immigration to the Land of Israel."

Chapter 16

She'eiris HaPleitah and Beyond

Sustainer of the Living

When it came to providing for the survivors' spiritual needs, nothing was too difficult for the Rebbe. After he had seen to reinstituting kosher slaughter and building a proper *mikveh*, he devoted his energy to establishing synagogues and yeshivos; acquiring and distributing sorely needed tzitzis, tefillin, and mezuzos; organizing a halachic framework for marriages and divorces; permitting *agunos* to remarry; and more.

Of the approximately 3,500 Jewish residents of the Foehrenwald DP camp itself, 1,983 identified themselves with the religious community,[1] which officially appointed the Klausenberger Rebbe as its rabbi and spiritual guide. But the Rebbe's efforts were not limited to helping the survivors in his own camp. In addition to leading the effort to reestablish Jewish

---

1 Reported by Dr. Hillel Zeidman in the Agudah newspaper *Kol Yisrael* (Jerusalem 1946).

life in the other twelve DP Camps in the American sector, the Rebbe traveled to camps and hospitals throughout the area, seeking out Jews who needed him.

Aryeh Avivi's description of his first encounter with the Rebbe clearly illustrates the Rebbe's activities on behalf of the survivors: "We were in the Funk Kaserne camp outside Munich, a huge international Displaced Persons camp. Thousands of people wandered around aimlessly. No one knew anyone else. People slept everywhere. There were beds above you and beds below you. The conditions were horrendous.

"There was one general cafeteria and we religious Jews would not eat there. We made do with stale bread and a little water. Then the Rebbe came, searching for lost Jews, and he found us. He came on his own. We had never even heard of him....

"He saw our suffering, took note of our condition, and left. A few days later he returned with several others carrying bulging bags of kosher sausage on their shoulders. They opened the bags immediately and began distributing the sausage to all the religious survivors."

The Lottery Winner

Once the Rebbe visited the Gauting Sanatorium outside Munich, a former German air force hospital which the Americans had turned into a hospital for concentration camp survivors. He brought with him a gift for the survivors — four packages of kosher tzitzis strings. The gift, however, proved to be insufficient — some 150 Jews stormed him, begging for the strings.

The Rebbe, seeing no alternative, suggested that a lottery be cast to determine who would get the strings. There was almost unanimous agreement — but one dissenting voice was heard. Mendel Pshitik, a young Gerrer chassid from Lodz, approached the Rebbe and asserted, "I should be given a package of tzitzis before anyone else!"

"Why?" asked the Rebbe. With a slight smile, he inquired, using a Talmudic phrase, "Is your blood redder than everyone else's?"

"Yes," answered the young man. As he spoke, he grabbed his shirt and, with two quick yanks, ripped it vertically on each side. "I am now wearing a garment of four corners which is required by Torah law to have tzitzis. No one else here is required by Torah law to wear tzitzis."

The Rebbe was visibly moved by the quick-witted survivor's action, but it had already been decided that a lottery would determine who received the tzitzis. After a moment's thought, he told the young man, "If your intentions are truly sincere, I am sure that you will win the lottery."

The tension was thick as the lottery was drawn. All the survivors longed for a precious packet of strings. Yet a joyous shout reverberated in the room when it was announced, "Mendel Pshitik is a winner!"[2]

The Tefillin that Saved a Dying Jew

Among the many stories of the Rebbe's devoted efforts to restore the spirituality of the survivors is the story of a chassid named Dovid Gottlieb. Dovid managed to remain observant throughout the Holocaust and with great effort succeeded in

---

2 Reported by Rabbi Moshe Gerlitz in *"HaGoral HaYehudi"* (The Jewish lot), in the book *Avihem shel Yisrael*, vol. 1, p. 93.

keeping a pair of kosher tefillin with him at all times. After he was liberated, he was hospitalized in an Austrian hospital. The doctors had all but given up hope for his recovery. Dovid continued to cling to his tefillin, which he kept under his pillow for safekeeping.

One day a friend visited him in the hospital. Seeing Dovid's frail state, he decided to take Dovid's tefillin with him so that they would not be desecrated by the non-Jewish hospital staff after Dovid's passing.

A short time later this friend came to Foehrenwald and met with the Rebbe. He related to the Rebbe how he had "saved" his friend's tefillin.

The Rebbe became extremely upset, sternly asking him, "How could you do such a terrible thing? Go back to Austria immediately and if this Jew is still alive give him back his tefillin."

The man did as he was told. When he reached the hospital, he found Dovid lying in his bed, alert but still in critical condition. He returned the tefillin to Dovid and conveyed the Klausenberger Rebbe's blessing for a speedy recovery. Suddenly, Dovid's condition began to improve. He experienced a miraculous return to health and eventually made aliyah.

"I did not know the Klausenberger Rebbe," Dovid Gottlieb would say, "but I feel I owe him my life."

Providing for New Couples

The Rebbe's efforts to restore the institution of marriage were substantial. "We are working with real self-sacrifice in this area," he wrote in a letter. "The mitzvah is very great, for everyone here is destitute and broken hearted."

The money needed to marry off new couples came from many varied sources. Shaul Hauterer, a Bobover chassid living in Antwerp, related: "After liberation from the cursed Mauthausen, I wandered with a few other Jewish survivors to Bregentz, a village in the French sector. From there we were sent to Hahenems, a small town in Austria that had apparently once housed a Jewish community. We began to rebuild the Jewish community as best we could, establishing Torah classes, prayer services, and so forth, but everything was on a very small scale.

"Then we heard about the community of religious Jews in Foehrenwald, and I made great efforts to get there. I went for one Shabbos and simply could not believe what I saw: A few short months after liberation, there were Jews with beards and *pei'os* celebrating Shabbos with the Klausenberger Rebbe! The davening and the *tisch* were intense, and the Rebbe's Torah lecture at the third Shabbos meal was extraordinary. There was a kosher *mikveh* and the beginnings of a yeshivah and a Bais Yaakov school for girls. I was awestruck.

"When I returned home, I remembered that I had a distant relative in Lugano, Switzerland, named Leibish Rubinfeld. My father had visited him once and told me that he was a great man. I quickly wrote this relative a letter (though I did not know his exact address) describing Foehrenwald, the Klausenberger Rebbe, and his many followers. I added that the survivors had nothing and were literally penniless.

"A few days later I received a telegram instructing me to come to the Swiss border. On the appointed day, I traveled to the border and met Leibish there. Leibish pleaded with the border police to allow us to speak for a few minutes over the border.

When no one was looking, he thrust a bag full of cash into my hand. 'Take this,' he said, and we quickly said our good-byes.

"The bag contained one thousand American dollars in twenty-dollar bills. I quickly set out for Foehrenwald, a six- or seven-hour journey, and related to the Rebbe that I had brought him money. He exclaimed joyously, 'With this money we will marry off ten couples during the next month.'

"And that is exactly what happened. I wrote to Leibish, thanking him for his generosity and asking him to send more money if possible. A couple of months later I received another telegram from him asking me to meet him at the border. This time he gave me five thousand dollars which he had collected from his family.

"I hurriedly left for Germany to give the money to the Rebbe. When I handed the bag to the Rebbe, he jumped for joy. 'Shaul, I am jealous of you! You have a part in the great mitzvah of providing for a bride! With this money we will be able to marry off fifty couples!'

"So it was. An announcement was made in the camp and the Rebbe promised to provide the basic needs for every religious bride and groom on the condition that the bride would cover her hair as required by halachah after her marriage. This was how the Rebbe established many religious Jewish homes."

Remarriages in the DP Camps

The Rebbe was also concerned with the plight of men and women who had no proof of the deaths of their spouses and therefore could not remarry. He tried to help them as much as he could, even though he did not have the *sefarim* necessary to research the complicated and difficult halachic issues involved in these cases.[3] In some instances the Rebbe permitted men to remarry based upon eyewitnesses' testimony that their wives had been selected in an Auschwitz lineup to be sent to the gas chamber. However, he was much stricter for himself, waiting two years after the war before remarrying and then obtaining a *heter mei'ah rabbanim*, a special Rabbinic decree, that he was permitted to remarry.[4]

The Rebbe was very hesitant to permit male survivors to marry their wives' surviving sisters based upon evidence that the wives had been in the lineup for the gas chambers because of the biblical prohibition against marrying two sisters. He wrote extensively on this subject in his responsa and discussed many reasons why he believed that it was possible to allow such marriages.[5] Nonetheless, because the issue involved a biblical, as opposed to a rabbinic, prohibition, he would not allow any marriages to take place before obtaining the concurring opinions of other Torah scholars living in Bucharest.

Eliyahu Reisman related, "One day the Rebbe received a letter from his dear friend Rabbi Chanoch Hillel Lichtenstein of Krosno, who was in the Landesberg DP camp. He proposed permitting a certain woman to remarry based upon sound halachic principles, reasoning, and evidence and asked the Rebbe to join in the ruling. The Rebbe, however, delayed responding to the letter for some unexplained reason.

"After some time had passed, Rabbi Lichtenstein wrote again, expressing his surprise that the Rebbe had failed to re-

---

3 Reported by Yeshayah Glick.
4 Reported by Yehoshua Veitzenblum.
5 Included in his *sefer Divrei Yatziv, Even HaEzer*.

spond to his original letter. A short time later, however, the allegedly dead husband appeared. He had actually survived the war and had been searching for his wife. The couple was reunited, and it then became clear why the Rebbe had not responded to Rabbi Lichtenstein's letter."

The First Yeshivah and Girls' School

The crowning glory of the Rebbe's work in Foehrenwald was the establishment of a central yeshivah for boys and young men, She'eiris HaPleitah, and a school for religious girls, Bais Yaakov. These two institutions saved literally hundreds of orphans from spiritual destruction. Because of them, the Rebbe was able to inform friends in Shevat 1946, a mere four months after his relocation to Foehrenwald, that "there were already hundreds of boys studying Torah and girls conducting themselves like Jewish daughters — something that would have been impressive even in earlier times and is especially so in today's situation."

As the father of all the orphans in the DP camps, the Rebbe viewed it his personal obligation to establish a yeshivah. The Rebbe obtained *sefarim* for the boys from American Jewish aid organizations, among them Vaad Hatzalah. He set up a dormitory and meals and selected excellent teachers. The Rebbe himself taught regular daily classes in Gemara and *Shulchan Aruch*. He began with simple lessons in Rashi and later developed more complex lectures, despite the lack of available *sefarim*. The Rebbe educated his students to live a life of Torah and fear of the Almighty, lifting them from the depths and eventually seeing many of them to the marriage canopy.

The Bais Yaakov for orphaned girls started with a small

number of girls who had been brought to the Rebbe in Feldafing from Bergen-Belsen. When the Rebbe moved to Foehrenwald and his name began to spread, refugee girls came to him from all over Germany and even from Poland, Czechoslovakia, and Hungary. The school grew to five grades with a student body of some 250 girls in a dormitory filled to capacity. Like Noach's ark, the school was a refuge for the girls from the spiritual flood around them. The Rebbe, who had lost his own daughters in the Holocaust, became a surrogate father to these hundreds of persecuted and depressed girls by providing them with a warm Jewish home in which they could recover both physically and spiritually from the war.

A Father's Blessing

As Yom Kippur of 1946 approached, Mrs. Abraham, the principal of the girls' school, came to the Rebbe with a request: "Isn't every Jewish girl entitled to a blessing from her father on *erev Yom Kippur*? Why should these girls have less just because they are orphans?"

The Rebbe was very moved and he acceded to the request, even though it was just before *Kol Nidrei*, one of the holiest moments of the year, when the Rebbe was normally enveloped in such fear of the Almighty that people were afraid to approach him. He instructed Mrs. Abraham to have all the girls approach the window of his room. Placing his hands, covered by a scarf, on the head of each girl, the Rebbe emotionally blessed each one in the memory of the holy souls who had perished in the Holocaust. Tears streamed down every face.[6]

---

6 Reported by Yehoshua Veitzenblum.

Beyond Foehrenwald

In response to the Rebbe's cry of "He who is for God, come to me!" a group of distinguished rabbis and lay leaders gathered together, committed to rebuilding religious Jewish life throughout the American sector. Working under the Rebbe's initiative and leadership, they established yeshivos and schools for girls in every DP camp. These educational institutions taught thousands of Jewish children Torah-true Judaism and provided for their material needs, as well, in an effort to prevent them from falling into the hands of the antireligious forces.

Soon the Rebbe expanded the operations of She'eiris HaPleitah and established Talmud Torahs and yeshivos in DP camps in Poking, Ulm, Feldafing, Wietersheim, Eichstatt, Landesberg, Bensheim, Bamberg, Krampek, and Eichnheilt. The Rebbe also set up one yeshivah in the French sector, located in Hahenems, Austria, near the French border, and supported a yeshivah called She'eiris Yisrael established in the British sector by his student Rabbi Yisrael Aryeh Zalmanovitz. In addition, the Rebbe oversaw the establishment of Bais Yaakov schools for girls in Wasserburg, Leipheim, Furth, Friemann, Schwebisch Hall, Ainring, and Wasseralfingen. More that twelve hundred girls received their education in these institutions. In some locations, youth chapters of Agudath Israel were also started.

In addition to the establishment of educational institutions, the Rebbe also created a central postwar Agudath Israel in Germany to advocate the interests of religious Jewry in the DP camps. The organization also published a religious newspaper in Hebrew and Yiddish.

Traveling to America

After Pesach of 1946, the financial situation of the religious community in the DP camps had become unbearable and the Rebbe decided to travel to America to raise funds. He also wanted to explore the options for emigration from Germany.

On June 21 (22 Sivan), at the end of Sivan, the Rebbe stepped foot on American shores for the first time. He spent seven weeks in New York, during which he touched the hearts of American Jews with his emotional prayer and electrifying *tische*s. Working tirelessly and speaking endlessly about the survivors' plight, he succeeded in raising $100,000, a huge sum in those days.

When he prepared to return to Europe after Tishah B'Av, his new chassidim begged him to stay in New York for a little while longer, but he had refused, saying that he was needed in Germany, especially for the upcoming high holidays.

On his way back to Germany the Rebbe stopped in Paris for ten days to attend to several matters on behalf of the survivors. When he reached Germany, three months after his departure to the United States, he was greeted joyfully by his followers, who had been assured by the irreligious elements in the camp that the Rebbe would never return.[7] The Rebbe, however, threw himself into his community work with even more vigor than before.

After Sukkos, the Rebbe prepared to leave for the United States again to continue raising money for the She'eiris HaPleitah institutions and to pave the way for his followers' and students' immigration. When his intentions became known, one of the Rebbe's followers expressed disappointment that the

---

7 Reported by Eliyahu Reisman.

Rebbe was immigrating to the United States and not to the Land of Israel. The Rebbe responded, "I am traveling to Eretz Yisrael by way of the United States."[8]

Later the Rebbe would explain that he had given considerable thought to whether the United States or the Land of Israel would be a better venue from which he could serve the Almighty. He remembered the vow he had made in the midst of his suffering that when he merited to leave the Nazi hell he would go to Eretz Yisrael.[9] In the end, however, he decided that Eretz Yisrael already had many great chassidic leaders, while America was a religiously barren land with much to be done there.[10] Thus, he had decided to go to America and satisfy his vow for the time being by working for the Holy Land from the United States.

A new chapter in the Rebbe's life had begun.

---

8 Reported by Meir Shraga Perdelsky.
9 See page 176.
10 Reported by Ben Tzion Reich, who heard it personally from the Rebbe.

The Sanz Dynasty

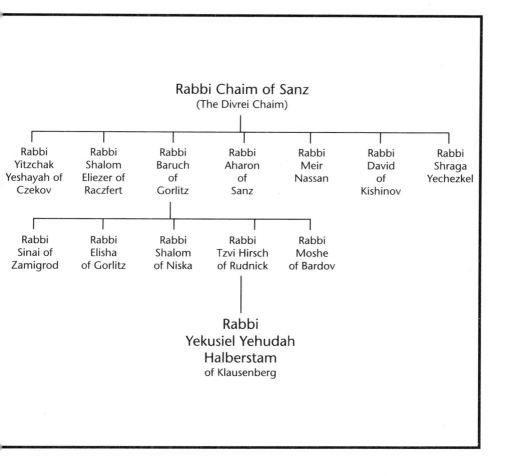

Rabbi Chaim of Sanz
(The Divrei Chaim)

| Rabbi Yitzchak Yeshayah of Czekov | Rabbi Shalom Eliezer of Raczfert | Rabbi Baruch of Gorlitz | Rabbi Aharon of Sanz | Rabbi Meir Nassan | Rabbi David of Kishinov | Rabbi Shraga Yechezkel |

| Rabbi Sinai of Zamigrod | Rabbi Elisha of Gorlitz | Rabbi Shalom of Niska | Rabbi Tzvi Hirsch of Rudnick | Rabbi Moshe of Bardov |

Rabbi
Yekusiel Yehudah
Halberstam
of Klausenberg

She'eiris HaPleitah Institutions

The Rebbe established many She'eiris HaPleitah institutions for the survivors in the displaced persons camps in western Europe, including:

- Talmud Torahs • yeshivos for young and old
- Bais Yaakov schools for girls
- dormitories and vocational schools for religious youth
- *kollels* • *hachnasas kallah* assistance organizations
- kosher kitchens • *mikvehs* • *bikur cholim* organizations

She'eiris HaPleitah institutions were established, among other places, in Hahenems, Austria; Bolei, France; and the following locations in Germany:

Ainring	Eichstatt
Bad-Reichenhall	Jager-Kaserne
Bamberg	Foehrenwald
Bensheim	Frian
Eichnheilt	Furth

Heidenheim   Schwebisch Hall
Krampek   Ulm
Landesberg   Wasseralfingen
Leipheim   Wasserburg
Munchen New Freimann   Wietersheim
Osvenga   Zeilsheim
Poking

In addition to these institutions, established under the Rebbe's leadership, the Rebbe assisted in raising large sums of money for many other religious institutions that were not officially part of the She'eiris HaPleitah network.